"Having grieved deeply condition of the church in America and much of the world, I have often cried out to God for revival and devoted most of my energies to this cause. Personally, I see no other hope for western civilization. That is why I am thrilled when books like this come out, and I am excited to recommend it! It is clear, concise, biblical and very inspirational. I pray that through it, you too will hear the cry of our Father's aching heart and help prepare the way for revival."

Dutch Sheets, senior pastor, Springs Harvest Fellowship,
Colorado Springs, Colorado;
author of *Intercessory Prayer* and *River of God*

"Many books have been written on revival. This book is different. First of all, there is what I call the touch of God on it. But second, it not only captures and imparts a passion and hunger for revival, it also carefully lays out the steps one must take to get there. I highly recommend this book as a guide for leading individuals, groups, churches and cities into revival. This is the day when God wants to bring whole nations to revival. This book is a must-read to help us get there."

Barbara Yoder, author of *The Breaker Anointing*

"As a teacher, Ian Malins is sound, solid, biblical, comprehensive and systematic in his analysis of 'revival.' But he is also a pastor-missionary and his passion is 'transformation' not just 'information.' From his own experience of personal and communal revivals, he seeks to show the way out of disappointing and stagnating evangelical 'religion' to a vibrant experience of intimacy with Jesus, which is the heart of revival movements and of authentic Christianity. Ian's clear conviction is that revival is the sovereign working of the Holy Spirit; nevertheless he itemizes a number of practical things that we can do to prepare ourselves for His coming."

Dr. Keith Hinton, doctor of ministry, director and professor of
Christian spirituality, Bible College of Victoria, Australia

"This book by Ian Malins has come to the Church at precisely the right time. Christians in the West concerned at the decreasing influence of Christianity are beginning to perceive the need for revival. A wave of prayer has commenced. But more than prayer is required. We need to understand the biblical principles by which God works. My personal experience as a leader in the Solomon Islands when revival swept the Church confirms that the lessons contained in this book are essential to any progress toward revival today. I recommend this book to all pastors and praying Christians."

Dr. John Tanner, director of The Pines Training Centre,
Southern Cross Ministries, Queensland, Australia

PREPARE THE WAY
for
REVIVAL

ESSENTIAL KEYS
THAT BRING GOD'S MANIFEST PRESENCE

IAN MALINS

Chosen
Grand Rapids, Michigan

© 2004 by Ian Malins

Published by Chosen Books
A division of Baker Book House Company
P.O. Box 6287, Grand Rapids, MI 49516-6287
www.bakerbooks.com

Printed in the United States of America

Library of Congress Cataloging-in-Publication Data

Malins, Ian.
    Prepare the way for revival : essential keys that bring God's manifest presence / Ian Malins.
        p.   cm.
    Includes bibliographical references and index.
    ISBN 0-8007-9373-0 (pbk.)
    1. Revivals. I. Title.
BV3790.M335 2004
269'.24—dc22   2003024167

To my wonderful wife, Diane,
and to my three special sons
—Dallas, Peter and David—
who have shared the journey with me.

In the desert prepare
the way for the LORD;
make straight in the wilderness
a highway for our God.

Isaiah 40:3

Contents

How to Use This Book

Personal Study

The chapters are short and easy to read. Read one chapter a day, which you may decide to use as the basis of your own devotional Bible study. Read the Bible passage at the end of each chapter and then in a separate notebook answer the questions. You may even benefit more by deciding to spend two days on each chapter so that you have time to complete the questions, meditate on what God is saying to you and let it go deep into your life. Ask God to help you apply what you are learning so that this becomes a life-changing journey for you.

After you have finished working through this book, review the chapters on a regular basis. This will keep your heart soft and open to the Holy Spirit's working in your life. Then use the book to help others in the same way. God is looking for a people prepared. As you prepare your own heart, you may find opportunities to help others prepare their hearts also.

Group Study

You will gain much more from the chapters, however, if you work through them with other Christians in small groups. You can be accountable to each other and share what you are learning together. Complete one chapter each week. The members of the group should complete the questions at the end of each study before coming to the group meeting so that they are properly prepared for the time of discussion. Read through the chapter together to get the topic in focus; then share your answers to the questions. Discuss what this means and ways of applying what you are learning. Pray together and encourage one another to apply the lessons, so that this will be a meaningful spiritual journey for each of you in the group.

INTRODUCTION

Probably at no other time in history has it been more exciting to be a Christian than now. The Holy Spirit is moving in ways never seen before. Across the world we are seeing thousands won daily into the Kingdom of God. And revival fires are touching and transforming Christians and churches in many countries.

Revival is a subject that continues to capture the attention of Christians everywhere. Most Christians listen to stories of revival with interest. Others talk about the great things God is doing in revivals across the world. Some even commit themselves to pray for revival. Why this great interest?

Perhaps it is because of the increasing number of reports we hear of revivals across the world and the desire to know more about what God is doing. Or because of the realization that we are living below God's best for us. There must be more to the Christian life than we are presently experiencing! We know deep within our hearts that we are not living up to the full potential God has for us. And there is a longing to know God more and live the kind of life the Scriptures say He intends for us. Is that true of you?

Scripture makes it clear that God has a great purpose for His people. He wants to make His Church a glorious, radiant Church so that as the darkness in the world increases, His light will shine even more brightly and unbelievers will be drawn to the Savior. But we know we are far from what we should be. So God has something far greater to do among us to bring us to this place. Perhaps that is why across the world, over the past decades especially, we have seen revivals on a scale never seen before. God is up to something big! He is awakening His people. He is breathing fresh life and vigor into them. He is preparing His Bride. He is reviving His Church. His light is penetrating the darkness. And despite the increase in evil, many believe we are seeing the beginnings of a mighty harvest of souls into the Kingdom that will take place before Christ comes again.

Prepare the Way for the Lord!

Jesus said, "I will build my church, and the gates of Hades will not overcome it" (Matthew 16:18). If that is what God is doing, what part do we have to play? Do we just sit back with folded arms and watch passively as events unfold? No! We are called to be part of His activity. Scripture makes it clear that we must prepare the way for the Lord. We do this first of all in our hearts, then in our homes and in our churches. Then His glory will be revealed to the nations.

Christians may differ in their views of what revival is, but the heart and center of revival is simply the rediscovery of the wonderful sense of the presence of God and a hunger for that presence. Both Scripture and revival history tell us clearly that God's manifest presence does not come automatically or easily (see Revelation 3:19–20). There are conditions to meet and preparations to make before God can come in revival blessing among us. Second Chronicles 7:14 is a key verse that tells us what these conditions are and how to prepare the way for the

Lord. Though spoken to King Solomon at the opening of the Jerusalem Temple, this verse gives us universal principles that apply to God's people in all generations. It is a well-quoted verse on revival, but how well is it understood and applied?

This is what we will explore through the pages of this book. We will look at Scripture and stories from past and present revivals and uncover step-by-step the keys that will transform your life, your church and our nation.

Do you really want revival? Do you want to be ready for all God desires to do in our time? Then begin to prepare the way for the Lord now. The chapters of this book will show you how.

PART 1

PREPARE THE WAY!

Scripture makes it clear that God has a great purpose for His people. He wants to bless us and make us a blessing to others. He wants to make His Church a glorious, radiant Church that will draw unbelievers to the Savior. If that is to take place, God has yet to do something far greater among us. And that is why across the world today we are seeing revivals on a scale never seen before.

For revival to come there are conditions we must recognize and preparations we must make. Revival is not a miraculous visitation of God falling upon an unprepared and unwilling people. We must prepare the way.

In the first two chapters of this book, we will look at what revival is and why we need it. We will hear again the call "Prepare the way for the Lord" and consider how to prepare the highway of our hearts. Then we will begin to do it. Are you ready for the journey? I want to be ready for all God is going to do. Don't you?

1

THE FIRE OF REVIVAL

*Revival is God bending down to the dying embers
of a fire just about to go out and breathing into it
until it bursts into flame.*

C. Evans

It was 1904 and Great Britain had drifted far from God. The spiritual conditions were very low. Church attendance was poor and sin abounded on every side. But unknown to each other, Christians all over Wales were calling out increasingly in prayer for God to intervene and send revival.

Suddenly, like an unexpected cyclone, the Spirit of God swept over the land. The churches were so overcrowded that many people were unable to get in. Meetings lasted from ten in the morning until midnight with several services held daily. Evan Roberts was the human instrument God used, but this was clearly a sovereign move of the Almighty. There was little preaching—singing, testimony and prayer were the main features. There were no hymnbooks. Most knew the hymns from childhood. There was no choir, for everyone sang. And there was no advertising. Yet people came from everywhere.

Nothing had ever come over Wales with such far-reaching results. Delinquents were converted; drunkards, thieves and gamblers saved; and thousands transformed. Drunkenness was immediately cut in half, and many taverns went bankrupt. Crime dropped so markedly that judges had no cases of murder, assault, rape or robbery to try. Old debts were repaid. Film theaters closed because no one showed up. Even the police in many districts had nothing to do and joined with the crowds going to the revival meetings. Heard on every side were confessions of awful sins and amazing testimonies of changed lives. In five weeks, twenty thousand people joined the churches. Within a year, that number had risen to one hundred thousand.

What Is Revival?

Some people think revival is powerful evangelism with many unbelievers coming to Christ and filling our churches. This may be the result of revival, but it is not where revival starts. The very word *revival* means to "re-vive" or "bring back to life again." *Revival* therefore has to do with reviving those who already have spiritual life (believers), whereas *evangelism* has to do with bringing life to those who have no spiritual life at all (unbelievers). Revival is what happens to the people of God; it is God re-viving and awakening His Church. It begins with the Church before it spills over into the world.

Christmas Evans, a famous Welsh preacher, says, "Revival is God bending down to the dying embers of a fire just about to go out and breathing into it until it bursts into flame."[1] Another writer, D. Panton, describes revival as "an inrush of divine life into a body threatening to become a corpse."[2]

Vance Havner says, "What we call revival is simply New Testament Christianity—the saints getting back to normal."[3]

J. Edwin Orr, using the words of Acts 3:19, defines revival as "times of refreshing from the presence of the Lord."[4]

Revival is God coming in His mercy to awaken us from spiritual sleep, to quicken us and raise us to the level of spiritual life we should always have been experiencing. Revival is God blowing upon the dying embers of our hearts to bring a fresh fire of love and passion for Him again. It is God coming

18

to stir up, refresh, renew and restore His people back to spiritual health, wholeness and joy in God. It is God bringing us back from subnormal to "normal" Christian life, back to New Testament Christianity.

What Happens When Revival Comes?

Pastor Joseph Kemp describes what happened when revival came to his church in Edinburgh in 1905:

> It was at a late prayer meeting, held in the evening at 9.30 that the fire of God fell. There was nothing, humanly speaking, to account for what happened. Quite suddenly, upon one and another came an overwhelming sense of the reality and awfulness of His presence and of eternal things. Life, death, and eternity seemed suddenly laid bare. Prayer and weeping began, and gained in intensity every moment. . . . One was overwhelmed. . . . Could it be real? We looked up and asked for clear directions, and all we knew of guidance was, "Do nothing." Friends who were gathered sang on their knees. Each seemed to sing, and each seemed to pray, without being aware of one another. Then the prayer broke out again, waves and waves of prayer; and the midnight hour was reached. The hours had passed like minutes. It is useless being a spectator looking on, or praying for it, in order to catch its spirit and breath. It is necessary to be in it, praying in it, part of it, caught by the same power, swept by the same wind. One who was present said: "I cannot tell you what Christ was to me last night. My heart was full to overflowing. If ever my Lord was near to me, it was last night."[5]

Revival history is full of stories like this. Again and again God has sent waves of revival to bring fresh life and vigor to His Church. But we don't have to look back to see these things happening: We just need to look around us now. Especially over recent decades we have seen revivals on a scale never known before in the history of the Church.

The Day of God's Visitation

What a sick and sleeping Church needs is not better programs, greater effort or even more teaching but a powerful visitation and revelation of God. Revival is simply that—God breaking into our churches and into our lives in a powerful, and perhaps unusual, way. It is God revealing Himself to us in awesome holiness and great power. This wakes us up. It shakes us out of our complacency. It stirs and challenges us deeply. It reveals those things in our lives that are stopping God from blessing His Church and using us. This part of revival is not what we like. It will be painful but is absolutely essential before God can come to us with the delights of His manifest presence.

James Burns in 1909 describes this part of revival in these words:

> To the church, a revival means humiliation, a bitter knowledge of unworthiness and an open humiliating confession of sin on the part of her ministers and people. It is not the easy and glorious thing many think it to be, who imagine it fills the pews and reinstates the church in power and authority. It comes to scorch before it heals; it comes to condemn ministers and people for their unfaithful witness, for their selfish living, for their neglect of the cross, and to call them to daily renunciation, to an evangelical poverty and to a deep and daily consecration. That is why a revival has never been popular with large numbers within the church. Because it says nothing to them of power such as they have learned to love, or of ease, or of success; it accuses them of sin; it tells them they are dead; it calls them to awake, to renounce the world and to follow Christ.[6]

Often we hear about revivals and think it is all glory and joy but don't realize that this deep cleansing must come first if revival is to be deep and lasting. Revival is first of all God coming to refine and purify His people so that we might burn for Him again with a pure and holy fire (see Malachi 3:1–5). This prepares us for the heart of revival, which is God restoring us to fellowship and intimacy with Himself because He loves us and then reaching out through us to people who are lost, broken and alienated from Him.

If this is what revival means, do you really want it? If you do, then journey with me through the following pages of this book and let God do in your life all He wants to do.

For Further Reflection

1. Read Psalm 85:1–13.
2. Look again at the account of the Welsh revival at the start of the chapter. Underline the words or sentences that clearly show that this was a sovereign move of God. How do you feel as you read this account?
3. Which parts of this chapter have spoken to you most clearly? Do you feel in some way you need to be renewed, restored and refreshed spiritually? What do you need?
4. Throughout Scripture we see people longing for more of God and longing for God to come in a greater way. What were the people in the following passages longing for? Psalm 85:4–9; Isaiah 64:1–9; Habakkuk 3:2.
5. Do you feel any of these same longings expressed in the above passages?
6. Now use the words of either Psalm 85 or Isaiah 64 to express the longings of your own heart to God. Read one or two verses at a time and then express the same thoughts back to God using your own words.

2

PREPARE THE HIGHWAY

*A baptism of holiness and a demonstration of
godly living is the crying need of our day.*

Duncan Campbell,
When the Mountains Flowed Down

Revival is a sovereign act of God, but, as already mentioned, God does not send revival blessings on a people unprepared for it. He will not pour out His Spirit on stony hearts, nor will He send His rain on those unready or unwilling to receive it.

In ancient times, when a king was to visit a city, a messenger would go before, telling the people to get ready. The people of that city would then get busy preparing the road along which the king would travel. They would remove rocks and stones on the road, fill in potholes and make the road wide and smooth. If these kinds of preparations were made for an earthly king coming to visit his people, how much more do we need to prepare the way for the sovereign Lord to come to us in divine visitation! In the desert and spiritually barren places, we need to begin now to prepare a straight highway so that the Lord can come to us. We need to do three things to make ready this highway.

Raise the Valleys

In making a highway, first we have to fill in the low places, the valleys and hollows, and raise them to the required level. Parts of our lives have sunk down, areas of decline where we have fallen short and are living far below God's best for us. These low areas may come about as a result of neglect of our spiritual lives, neglect of our family lives, neglect of relationships, disobedience, unconfessed sins, failure, hurt, unforgiveness or other such things.

In preparing the way for God to come in revival, these areas must be dealt with. We need to recognize them and admit that they are hindering God's purpose and preventing Him from coming in renewing fullness to us. We must confess them and ask for His help to deal with them. Then He delights to come and help us. If you feel unworthy, unaccepted or unloved by God because of painful experiences, you need to come to a fresh understanding of God's unconditional love for you and His total acceptance of you. Where there are unhealed wounds in your life, you may need to open your heart for His healing touch. You need to realize afresh how much God loves you, what He has done for you and who you really are in Christ. Every valley must be raised and every low area built up so that the Lord can come in power and blessing. Are you ready to begin with God the work of building up these sunken areas of your life?

Level the Hills

To make a straight and level highway for the Lord, we must not only build up the low places, but we must cut through any high mountains and hills and bring them down to the right level. Boulders and rocks in the way must be broken or removed.

The mountains and hills speak of the hard, resistant areas in our lives we must deal with before the Lord can come to us in revival—things like pride, unbelief, resistance to the Holy Spirit, self-will, self-effort, self-righteousness, a critical spirit and other such things. These are obstacles to the knowledge and presence of God that prevent Him from coming to us in all His fullness. Often we do not recognize these things in our lives. Pride in all its various forms is a very deceitful thing that we may see in others but not in ourselves. Yet these things can block and hinder God's deeper work within us without our realizing it. The spirit of pride must be dealt with in our lives, and we must be brought to a place of brokenness, submission and humility before the Lord. Only then can we make a highway for the Lord in our hearts that is clear of obstacles and hindrances so that He can come to us.

Make the Rough Places Smooth

When the low places are built up and the high places brought down, the final part of preparing a highway is to grade and roll the rough and bumpy surface of the road to make it completely even and smooth.

The uneven areas of our lives speak of the inconsistencies in our Christian living—the ups and downs, the hot and cold, the rough places where we still need further refining to make our lives smooth and straight. Are you harsh in your relationships with others—your wife, husband, children or family members? Are you impatient, irritable, unfair or unkind in your dealings with others? These rough areas must be made smooth. It is the work of the Spirit in our lives to produce in us the consistent qualities of Christlike character and behavior. But we must ask Him to deal with the jagged reactions and responses of our self-life and replace them with the even responses of the Spirit-filled life (see Galatians 5:22–23).

How level and smooth is the highway of your heart? How consistent are the marks of the Spirit-filled life seen in your life every day? This will not be done through self-effort, though you must do your part. Only the Spirit within you can level the uneven places. So you must cooperate with Him in the pressures and problems of everyday life, denying the self that wants to react and rise up and asking the Spirit of Jesus to live through you instead.

Then the Glory of the Lord Will Be Revealed

When the low places have been built up, the high places brought down and the rough places made smooth, then

> the glory of the LORD will be revealed,
> and all mankind together will see it.

> Isaiah 40:5

God wants to come in these last days with a mighty outpouring of His Spirit and a fresh revelation of His glory before all people. But this begins with those who call themselves Christians. Only when we are living holy lives will the world be confronted with the holiness of God. "Then the nations will know that I am the LORD, declares the Sovereign LORD, when I show myself holy through you before their eyes" (Ezekiel 36:23). Though these words were originally spoken to the Jewish people, they continue to speak of God's purpose for His people of every age (see Matthew 5:16). We may be in the wilderness and desert places now, but when the highway of holiness is prepared the Lord will come in glory and power to His people. And all people will see it together (both believers and unbelievers) and be deeply affected by it. But are you ready? Is the highway prepared? Or are there still low places, obstacles and rough areas that need to be dealt with? It's time now to prepare the way for the Lord!

For Further Reflection

1. Read Isaiah 40:3–5. According to this passage, what kinds of preparations need to be made so that God can come in divine visitation to His people? What does this mean?
2. What has God been saying to you personally through reading this chapter? What must you do to prepare in your heart a highway for the Lord?
3. Look at the marks of the Spirit-filled life seen in Galatians 5:22–23. How consistently are these seen in your life every day?
4. When the low places have been built up, the high places brought down and the rough places made smooth, what has God promised will happen (see Isaiah 40:5)? What does this mean for us today?
5. Think about the quote at the start of the study and read Ezekiel 36:23. What has God been saying to you personally about the condition of the highway of your heart? Where do you need to begin and what can you start to do this week?

PART 2

THE CONDITIONS
OF REVIVAL

Second Chronicles 7:14 clearly tells us that there are divine conditions that must be met before God will send revival and bring healing to our land. Revival does not happen any way; it happens God's way. And God's way is clearly spelled out in this verse:

If my people, who are called by my name, will

- *humble themselves (brokenness)*
- pray (dependence)
- seek my face (intimacy)
- turn from their wicked ways (repentance)

Then will I

- hear from heaven
- forgive their sin
- heal their land

The first condition of revival is to *humble ourselves*. Those who long for revival often pass over this first condition without realizing what it means. The root of sin is *pride*. We must first deal with the self-life that rules within. Before we can experience revival, the pride in our hearts must be broken. We will look at what this means in the next two chapters.

3

Our Greatest Problem— Pride

> *The most essential commodity for stimulating revival is a tender, open heart before God.*
>
> Francis Frangipane, *The House of the Lord*

Pride in its many forms is the first and greatest blockage to revival. It is like the mountains and hills and the boulders that block the Lord's highway. These must be broken down and cleared away before God can come to us in divine visitation. The first condition of revival is humility.

Pride is the chief sin that spoils our relationships with God and with others. It spoiled our first parents at the start of human history. And ever since that time pride has been the root of all our problems. It shows itself in independence and self-centeredness. It stops us from recognizing our total dependence on God. It keeps us from enjoying close fellowship with Him. And it is the chief cause of the conflicts between people. It spoils our lives, our families and our churches. That is why it must be dealt with first before we can go any further.

Pride in Ourselves

Pride makes us think we can manage by ourselves. Even as Christians this root of independence, self-sufficiency and self-centeredness can influence our Christian lives. It colors our attitudes and our actions. We give little time to prayer. We try to live the Christian life by our own efforts. We may be busy in Christian service and active in serving the Lord. Yet we may still be doing it our way rather than God's way. We may depend on our own efforts rather than on the Holy Spirit and do what we think best rather than seeking His mind and perfect will.

Pride also causes us to measure our value or worth against others rather than seeing our true value in God's sight. This leads either to feelings of superiority or to inferiority. It makes us think, "I am better than you" or "I am less than you." Instead of our mutual sense of dependence on God drawing us together, pride drives us apart. It puts barriers between us and leads to all kinds of relationship problems.

You may be proud of your abilities, your gifts or achievements. You may be proud of your position in the church, your reputation or the way God has used you. Yet at other times you may feel inferior or less than others. Inferiority is not humility; it is hurt pride, the underside of superiority. It can make you jealous or envious of others, critical and competitive (even in Christian ministry) and quick to put others down. Inferiority can also make you self-conscious, reserved and oversensitive. When you hold resentment and unforgiveness in your heart, this is a sign of wounded pride.

Before we can know revival, God has to deal with our proud hearts. Our proud self-life must be broken. In other words, we must die to self and self-attitudes before we can be filled with the life and love of Jesus.

Pride in Our Churches

Pride may not only be a personal thing; it can also be a corporate thing. We may be proud of *our* church. We may be proud of *our* denomination. We can think our denomination is better than other denominations, or our church is better than other churches. We can be proud of our buildings, our size, our preaching, our emphasis on the Word of God, our style of worship, our music, our outreach programs, our community care, our giving to missions or other things. We can think our church is achieving more than other churches. We can think our church is more Christ-centered and closer to the truth. We can think we are more spiritual or have more of the Holy Spirit. We may even think that if God is going to bring revival to our area, our city or our nation, it will surely be through *our* church!

Dr. Sangster, a Methodist leader in England, writes these challenging words:

> We have boasted—in all denominations—of our traditions. "Ours is the only church which really goes back to the Apostles. Ours is the established church. . . . Our church is truly Bible-based." Is there nothing of pride in all this? Are we implying that we are more dear or near to God than his other blood-bought sheep?[1]

Before revival can come, God has to deal with this corporate pride within us. The barriers between churches have to be broken down. God has no favorites. When we humble ourselves as churches and begin praying for one another instead of just for ourselves, we will see God beginning to work. When we confess our neglect and pride and begin seeking unity and reconciliation across the Body of Christ, we open the channels for revival to come. God is not just concerned to revive our church; He has a much bigger plan. He wants to revive *His* Church. So we had better get this bigger picture!

Pride in Our Ministry

Pride not only affects the average church member; it can also affect those who serve and lead. In fact, there is an even greater danger of pride for those who have public ministry gifts and responsibilities. Those in ministry can be proud of their positions within the church. They can be proud of their gifts, their influence, their achievements or the results of their ministry. If there is any success, they want to get some credit for it, or talk as if they did it.

When A. W. Tozer attended a conference at one time, he listened with patience day after day as pastors and preachers told of what they had done, how far they had traveled in ministry and how God was mightily using them. Finally, when his turn came to preach, Tozer got up and rebuked the boasters with his opening words. He said, "I am tired of coming to conferences to watch men strut!"[2]

If we are wondering why revival is still a long way off, then one of the key reasons is right here. The Church is full of people who want status, position, power, rather than desiring to serve. They want the recognition and praise of others. They want to be in the spotlight. They want control. But God will not come in revival blessing to any people who are going to take His glory for themselves.

Henry Morehouse was a young minister greatly used of God to bring many people to Christ in revivals in England and America. In one of his meetings, nothing much was happening. He gave himself to earnest prayer. "O God," he cried, "why am I not preaching with freedom and power? Why are the people so unresponsive? Why are so few being saved?"

God gave him the answer to his questions as he walked down a street. On a large billboard he read some flattering words about himself: "Hear the most famous of all British preachers—Henry Morehouse!" God seemed to say to him, "That's why there is no revival." He went immediately to those in charge of the meetings and said:

> No wonder there is no revival. No wonder the Holy Spirit cannot work. You have advertised me as the greatest this

32

and the greatest that. The Spirit is grieved because we have not magnified the Lord Jesus Christ and given all the glory to His mighty Name. He is the wonderful One. I am only a voice saying, "Behold the Lamb of God."[3]

L. E. Maxwell, in his book *Born Crucified,* says:

> The church is full of ministers, Sunday school teachers and workers, evangelists and missionaries, in whom the gifts of the Spirit are very manifest and who bring blessing to multitudes, but who, when known close up, are found to be full of self. They may have "forsaken all" for Christ and imagine they would be ready, like the disciples of old, to die for their Master; but deep down in their hidden private lives, there lurks that dark sinister power of *self.*[4]

Pride in Our Experiences of God

Pride can infect our spiritual lives. We may be proud of the way God has worked in us. We may be proud of our spiritual experiences or the gifts God has given us. This is *spiritual* pride. Feelings of superiority can easily slip in unnoticed and develop the attitude "I am more spiritual than you." Those who have certain gifts of the Spirit may look down on those who haven't and regard them as second-class Christians. How wrong this is, and how it grieves the Spirit of God!

Paul Smith makes this comment:

> God cannot use the Christian who has begun to look down upon other Christians. There is no greater hindrance to revival than the person who feels he has attained spiritually and now stands head and shoulders above his brethren in the Lord. The person who has a consciousness of his own superiority in the things of the Spirit is a powerless Chris-

tian. The Christian who is proud is not spiritual and the Christian who is spiritual is not proud.[5]

Being proud of our spiritual gifts or experiences in God is not the way of the Spirit. Rather, it shows that the self-life is still in control. The way of the Spirit is always humility. We are undeserving of all that God has done for us, so how can we be proud or boast about it (see 1 Corinthians 4:7)?

The Answer to Pride: Brokenness

We cannot deal with pride simply by trying to be more thoughtful of others. The self-life must die before Christ can fill our lives with His presence. Pride has to be broken. Like rocks and boulders blocking the highway, pride must be smashed, broken down and removed. We cannot begin to walk in humility until this has happened.

Usually when we think of something broken, we think of it as spoiled—a broken plate, window, watch. These things have become useless. But this is not what brokenness means when applied to our lives. A better way to think of brokenness is in terms of hard, stony ground that needs to be broken up, cleared of stones and plowed in readiness to receive seed and rain. Only this kind of preparation will make the soil deep and soft to produce a bountiful harvest. The same is true of our lives.

Brokenness is when we realize that everything we have is because of God's mercy and grace. There is nothing we can claim as of ourselves. We are unworthy and unfit to be loved or used by God. Yet He does love us and has chosen to use us. So there is nothing we can be proud of or boast of except of what God has done. God cannot fully use us until there is this kind of brokenness. That is the first condition of revival! Are you ready for it?

For Further Reflection

1. The following passages tell us that God looks with favor and revives what kind of people? Psalm 51:17; Isaiah 57:14–15; 66:2; 1 Peter 5:5–6.
2. Look back at the main points of this chapter and think about the condition of your own heart before God. How much of self is there? How much pride is in each of these areas? What is God saying to you?
3. The answer to pride is brokenness. What do you think "brokenness" means? How does it apply to you personally?
4. Respond to God in prayer using the words of Ezekiel 36:25–27, asking God to remove any stony areas and to give you a heart of flesh.

4

The First Condition— Humility

To be broken is the beginning of revival. It is painful, it is humiliating, but it is the only way.

Roy Hession, *The Calvary Road*

It was annual conference time for a group of missionaries in the highlands of Papua New Guinea. I had been asked to be the speaker and with my wife shared in ministry over several days. These missionaries were very tired and discouraged and were experiencing serious relationship problems among themselves. At the final Communion service, as I was about to pass around the bread and the wine, the mission leader interrupted and said he needed to say a few words first. He stood up and confessed to his fellow missionaries that he had had wrong attitudes toward each of them over the past year. He said how God had convicted him of this, and he needed to put this right before taking Communion. He then went around the circle of missionaries one by one asking for forgiveness and saying to each of them, "I love you in Jesus." Something broke within that group of missionaries and tears began to flow freely. One by one, different ones got up and began to confess things they had against each other and asking for forgiveness. This continued for over half an hour as the Holy Spirit took over and did His cleansing work. I sat back and watched in amazement what God was doing. There was brokenness and there were tears. Forgiveness and reconciliation flowed, and deep wounds were healed that day. What a powerful sense of the presence of God filled that room as they confessed their sins to one another and put things right! Truly what we were witnessing that day was the start of revival among this group of weary and disheartened missionaries.

If pride is the first main obstacle to revival, then how do we deal with it? Second Chronicles 7:14 gives us the simple answer: "If my people, who are called by my name, will *humble themselves*" (emphasis added). God tells us to humble *ourselves*. It is no use praying, "Lord, make me humble." Coming to a place of humility is something *we* must do. Even though we cannot do it without Him, God does not do it for us. So it is our choice whether we become humble and tender in heart or remain proud and self-centered.

How Do We "Humble Ourselves"?

How, then, do we humble ourselves to develop a tender and contrite heart toward God and others? There are five main ways.

We humble ourselves by praying and seeking God's face

Pride makes us think we can manage our lives and our churches on our own. So we work hard and pray little. But 2 Chronicles 7:14 tells us clearly that God will not work powerfully among us until we humble ourselves and pray and seek His face. We must recognize our total dependence on God for everything. We must realize we can do nothing without Him. More than that, we must be desperate for Him. Sometimes this desperation is accompanied by fasting. We have tried so hard and seen so little. Now we know nothing will really change unless God intervenes and sends revival. And so we humble ourselves before Him and cry out to Him to come and meet us in our need. This humbling before God in earnest prayer has always been a part of revivals in the past. And it still is a condition of revival today. Has your church come to this place yet? Have you?

We humble ourselves by coming before God with a contrite heart

It is one thing to pray and seek God's face, but it is another to come before God with the right attitude of heart. Even in the act of praying, we can come before God in the wrong way. We can come with a proud and self-sufficient heart: "Lord, I'm all right, but please change these other people!" And even in the act of fasting, when we are supposedly humbling ourselves before God, pride can rear its ugly head and destroy the very purpose for which we fast. We can become more focused on our fasting (and on ourselves) than on seeking God's face and focusing on Him. And we can secretly want others to know we are fasting so that they will think more highly of our spiritual devotion. No wonder Jesus warned His disciples when they fasted to keep this strictly a secret between themselves and God alone (see Matthew 6:16–18). It is too easy for pride to get in!

God will only respond in favor to the person who comes before Him with a humble and contrite heart (see Luke 18:9–14). It is not what you pray but *how* you pray that matters. You may spend hours in prayer, bringing your requests to God. You may fast for many days. But if you come without a humble and repentant heart, it is all for nothing. How often have we come to God in prayer, yet gone away untouched and unchanged because we have come full of ourselves? We have come with our own interests, our own plans, our own desires, our own requests but have not humbled ourselves, have not sought His face, have not dealt with the pride that lurks within and have not repented of the things He has wanted to reveal to us.

Duncan Campbell, who was a part of the Hebrides revival in Scotland in 1949, tells the story of a group of people praying in a barn and kneeling on the straw. One of them, a young deacon, opened up his Bible and read from Psalm 24:3–4:

> Who may ascend the hill of the LORD?
> Who may stand in his holy place?
> He who has clean hands and a pure heart.

After reading the passage twice, the young man said, "Brethren, it is just so much humbug to be waiting thus night after night if we are not right with God. I must ask myself: 'Is my heart pure? Are my hands clean?'" He got no further but fell prostrate to the floor. An awareness of God filled the barn and a stream of supernatural power was let loose in their lives. They had moved into a new sphere of God-realization ... and that was the start of revival.[1]

When did you last come before God with a broken and contrite heart? The story of revivals both past and present shows that a spirit of humility, godly sorrow and repentance always comes before a move of God in blessing and power.

We humble ourselves by confessing our faults to one another

One of the clear conditions of revival is the open and honest confession of sin and the desire to put wrongs right. Undealt-with grievances cause division, disunity and alienation in our homes and churches. Pride stops us from owning our sins, confessing our wrongs and putting things right. It destroys our families and divides our churches. It keeps wounds unhealed. But healing will come only when we humble ourselves and take the first step to admit our wrongs, to confess our faults, to apologize, to repent of our actions, to seek forgiveness and to change our ways (see Matthew 5:23–24; James 5:16). To admit our wrongs before others is very humbling! But that's exactly what is needed to break pride and develop humility within us. Are you willing to apologize where that is needed—to your wife, your husband, your children, your parents or to those within the family of God? Once sin is brought out into the light, it can be properly dealt with—its power has been broken. This humbling before others is the key that opens the door for the Spirit to work deeply in our lives and among God's people. And that is exactly what is needed for revival to come!

We humble ourselves by being willing to forgive

It is humbling to have to confess our wrongs to others and seek their forgiveness. But what do we do when someone has wronged or hurt us? Our natural reaction is to stand on our pride and insist that the offense be dealt with. But to forgive means to die to the self-life that cries out for justice and revenge. Our human nature would rather keep others in debt to us and make them pay for what they have done. But to release them through forgiveness requires divine grace and true humility. Think about Jesus as He was physically abused, unjustly treated and nailed to the cross. He was the Son of God, yet He didn't curse, scream and threaten those who so humiliated and mistreated Him (see Luke 23:34; 1 Peter 2:23). Instead, He offered forgiveness to those who didn't deserve it or even ask for it! And, hard as it is, and so opposite to the self-life within, Jesus calls us to do the same (see Matthew 6:14–15).

Pride makes us nurse our hurts and want to keep the wrongdoer in our debt. But it takes great humility in the face of wrong to be willing to release the person from our anger and offer forgiveness instead. And when we release a person, we also are released, for healing comes through forgiveness.

The healing power of forgiveness

When you have been wrongly treated, releasing forgiveness is like ointment on your wound. Jesus forgave those who crucified Him. And He gives you the grace to forgive those who have wronged and hurt you. Holding unforgiveness in your heart will block the flow of God's grace and forgiveness into your life and hinder your healing. It will hurt you more than the person who has wronged you. So get rid of it for your own sake! Release the person from your anger and you, too, will be set free. Release people to God and let Him deal with them (see Romans 12:19). When you forgive, you will know God's forgiveness also. And when those feelings return (as they most probably will), keep applying more ointment to the wound by repeatedly forgiving them. Your wound may remain tender for some time, the hurt may still be there, but gradually you will know the deep healing only God can bring.

Francis Frangipane says:

> The redemptive power of God is released when people forgive each other. Individuals, families, churches and even the atmosphere of a city can change when pardon is released. . . . It is the river of life flowing again into the cold, hardened valleys of a once-embittered heart. Forgiveness is at the core and is the essence of revival itself.[2]

We humble ourselves by serving one another

Philippians 2:7 tells us that Jesus humbled Himself by "taking the form of a servant." Jesus, knowing who He really was (the Son of God) and knowing where He would soon return (back to the place of highest glory and honor), humbled Himself and took a towel—stooping to do the work of a slave (see John 13:1–17)! This was something the proud disciples would never have done for each other. Yet Jesus did it for them.

It requires humility to put others first and willingly serve them. Yet this is what living in the Kingdom is all about. Our pride makes us think others should serve us. But when we are willing to humble ourselves by taking every opportunity to serve others in love (even though others may not notice it), we open our lives to the rivers of blessing and revival that flow from God's presence.

For Further Reflection

1. Read Isaiah 57:14–19.
2. In this chapter we have looked at five main ways we humble ourselves. Check yourself against each one. Are these weak, moderate or strong in your own life?
3. When we humble ourselves like this, we open the door to revival. Why is this? What do the following references tell us? Psalm 51:16–17; Isaiah 57:14–19; 66:1–2.
4. Read Micah 6:8. Pause and think for a few minutes about your relationships. Look again at the five main points in the chapter. How do you relate to God and to others? On the basis of pride or in humility? Ask God to reveal to you anything in these areas you need to do this week. Write it down and then do it.

PART 3

A PASSION
FOR GOD'S PRESENCE

We have looked at the first essential step toward revival—humbling ourselves. Now we move on to the
second condition of revival, as outlined in 2 Chronicles 7:14:

If my people, who are called by my name, will

- humble themselves (brokenness)
- *pray (dependence)*
- seek my face (intimacy)
- turn from their wicked ways (repentance)

Then will I

- hear from heaven
- forgive their sin
- heal their land

Before we can expect revival, God's people must *pray*. Prayer always prepares the way for revival. Prayer shows our dependence on God. Without seeking Him, nothing will happen. We can be absolutely certain that when revival comes, it is because some have been willing to pay (or pray) the price. We will look at what this means over the next three chapters.

5

A HUNGER FOR GOD'S
PRESENCE

The greatest single aspect of every true revival is
the peculiar and wonderful sense of the presence
of God.

Richard Owen Roberts, *Revival*

No one could describe exactly what happened on that August morning in Herrnhut, Germany, in 1727. As three hundred Moravian believers gathered together for a specially called Communion service, a strange power over-shadowed them and a spirit of conviction fell upon them. At first there was an awesome silence, then muffled sobs, then overflowing tears and cries. Grievances were confessed, sins repented of and reconciliations made. The fire of God fell, and the glory of the Lord came upon those people so power-fully that they hardly knew if they were on earth or in heaven. Tears and forgiveness flowed freely, and the great Moravian revival had begun.

One of the Moravians described the effects of this divine visitation in these words:

A great hunger after the Word of God took possession of us so that we had to have three services every day. . . . Every one desired above everything else that the Holy Spirit might have full control. Self-love and self-will, as well as all disobedience,

45

disappeared and an overwhelming flood of grace swept us all out into the great ocean of Divine Love.[1]

What is the center of revival? Is it confession of sin? Is it signs and wonders? Is it joy and excitement? Is it strange phenomena? All these may be part of revival, but they are not the center. The center of revival is a rediscovery of the "wonderful sense of the presence of God" and a hunger for that presence. It is the wakening of the desire within us to know God more. It is the stirring up of a passion and longing for a deeper intimacy with Christ. Duncan Campbell, who was part of the revival in Scotland in 1949, describes revival simply as "a community saturated with God."[2]

Three Kinds of Hunger

There are three kinds of spiritual hunger. The *first* is probably not really hunger at all. Some Christians have never experienced in their lives or churches the powerful presence of God seen in revival. They believe that what they now know of God's presence is all there is. As a result, they are happy to stay within their present limited experience of God and may even reject revival as unnecessary, extreme or unbiblical.

The *second* kind of hunger is for something we have never experienced before but long for. Many Christians who have never sensed the powerful presence of God seen in revival have nevertheless heard of it and yearn for it. They know God has more for them than they have yet experienced and they hunger for more of Him.

The *third* kind of hunger is for something we have already experienced but have lost. Some Christians have known the powerful presence of God in revival. They have had sweet intimacy with Jesus but for various reasons have lost it. Now they have a deep desire to return to where they once were.

46

Three Dimensions of God's Presence

In talking about the presence of God, we must understand
that in Scripture there are three different levels or dimensions
of God's presence. First, there is God's *general presence.* God
is everywhere, so no matter where we are, He is there also.
We cannot escape from His Spirit (see Psalm 139:7–12). His
presence fills the whole universe. But more than that, our very
life and existence depend upon His constant presence and
sustaining power (see Hebrews 1:3). An external presence of
God surrounds all people (like the air), whether we realize it
or not. And without this general presence we could not even
exist (see Acts 17:28).

Second, there is God's *indwelling presence.* This is a deeper
dimension of God's presence that we experience at the time of
spiritual birth (see John 3:5). Before we believed and received
Christ, we were spiritually dead. There was no spiritual life
within us. But when we believed, we were brought into cov-
enant relationship with God, and His Spirit is now not only
with us but dwells within us (see John 14:17). Some Christians
go only this far in their understanding of God's presence. But
there is more to His personal presence than that (as wonderful as that is!).

Third, there is God's *manifest presence.* Jesus speaks about
this in John 14:21 when He says, "I too will love him and show
[manifest] myself to him." The manifest presence of Jesus is
not just the presence of Jesus living within us; it is the presence
of Jesus revealed among us. It is God visiting His temple (both
individually and corporately). It is God's Spirit moving in us,
among us and upon us in holiness and power. It is a presence
we can feel. At such times people know without a doubt that
God is in their midst, moving and touching their lives. This is
the level of God's presence we experience especially in times
of revival. And many have never known this kind of presence
before.

God in the Midst

Revival is a time when God is in the midst of His people in His manifest presence. It is a time when the Spirit of Jesus moves freely and reveals Himself in a very personal and powerful way. But some may say, "Isn't the presence of Jesus an automatic thing? Isn't Christ always in the midst of His people?"

God may be in His individual temple (our individual lives), but He may not be in His corporate temple (the assembled body of believers). Revelation 3:20 makes that clear. These words are not spoken to individuals; they are spoken to a church. While the believers at Laodicea were on the inside having their worship service, Jesus was on the outside knocking on the door wanting to come in! Jesus' manifest presence was not with them! Why? Because they had neglected their love relationship with Him, had become proud and complacent and had grieved His Spirit. But if they would repent of their lukewarmness and pride, love Him again as they did at first and open the door to His presence, Jesus would come to them again with His manifest presence. This is how He also longs to come to us. And when He does, what fellowship, what joy and what intimacy as He speaks and reveals Himself to us!

A Passion for More of God

The heart of revival is to restore the manifest presence of Jesus. As we look through the Scriptures, we see people hungry for more of God and with a passion for His presence. Moses wanted above everything else God's presence, not just His blessings (see Exodus 33:13–16). The psalmists also expressed their longing for the place of God's presence and glory (see Psalm 84:1–2). Paul's primary passion was to know Christ more deeply and intimately (see Philippians 3:7–10). The word *passion* (Greek, *pathos*) speaks of something that deeply stirs us, drives us, compels us and is something we long for. The opposite of passion (Greek, *apathos*) is apathy, which means nothing stirs us—we do not care and are uninterested.

How is your passion for God? Many Christians seek God's hand (His blessings) rather than seeking His face (His presence). Many have lost or never had a passion for God Himself. Other things have drained it away. But when we are awakened to realize we have lost the most important thing of all, and when we deal with the reasons for our loss, God delights to draw near to us again with His wonderful manifest presence. And when He does, what glory and what joy! That is revival indeed!

For Further Reflection

1. Read Exodus 33:12–23.
2. Reread the story of the Moravian revival at the start of the study. What are the central elements of revival we see in this story? What impresses you most?
3. Think again about the three kinds of spiritual hunger mentioned in this chapter. Which do you most closely relate to?
4. Look up the following references. What level of God's presence is each talking about? Psalm 139:7–10; John 14:21; 1 Corinthians 6:19–20. Which of the above levels of God's presence have you experienced?
5. Look at the following examples of people who had spiritual hunger for more of God. What was each person longing for? Moses (Exodus 33:13–18); the psalmist (Psalm 42:1–2); David (Psalm 63:1–3); the psalmist (Psalm 84:1–2); Paul (Philippians 3:10).
6. Which of the above biblical examples most closely reflects the hunger for God you feel? Use the words of one of these passages to guide you in prayer expressing how you feel to God.

6

PRAYER AND REVIVAL

*When God intends a great mercy for His people,
the first thing He does is set them a-praying.*

Matthew Henry,
Matthew Henry's Commentary on the Bible

The great Moravian revival was preceded and followed by most extraordinary praying. Nicholas von Zinzendorf, who was the leader of the Moravian community, was a young man 27 years old. He was discouraged and deeply burdened by the lack of spiritual life in his followers. They were troubled by disunity, criticisms and deep divisions. He was also deeply burdened for the nine schoolgirls in his Bible class. So he began to pray and agonize for these people. What a picture! A gifted, wealthy young German nobleman on his knees agonizing in prayer for the divided community of believers and for the conversion of these girls! Soon he was spending hours, days and nights in earnest intercession. Often his prayers were accompanied with a flood of tears as he poured out his heart to God.

This prayer produced extraordinary results as the Holy Spirit began to work in a new way. It was not long before many others began to pray as never before. A group of about twelve or fourteen covenanted together of their own accord to meet and pray with von Zinzendorf. Soon they were gathering regularly, pouring out their hearts to God in prayer and worship. On August 5 they spent the whole night in prayer and prayed with great passion. On August 13, 1727, when three hundred had assembled for a Communion service, the Holy Spirit fell upon them, bringing deep conviction, repentance and reconciliation.

The Need for Prayer

A passion for God's presence begins in the place of prayer. No Christian can expect to know God intimately without seeking Him in prayer. And no church can ever expect revival unless it prays for it. This does not mean that revival will not come to such a person or such a church, for God is sovereign and cannot be limited. But prayer is the avenue through which God works. So you can be sure that when revival comes, it comes because someone, somewhere has prayed for it.

Studying the great revivals of the past will show that every revival is closely connected with powerful, believing, intercessory prayer. Prayer is both the cause and the result of the coming of the Spirit in revival. When God's people give themselves to prayer, God works. When they do not pray, nothing much happens. Prayer does not cause revival to come in an automatic way, but it prepares the way for revival to come when God chooses to send it.

What Will Bring Us to Our Knees?

If prayer is the channel through which revival comes, then what will bring us to pray? Proud Christians don't want to pray—it is too humbling. Complacent Christians don't see the need to pray—they are happy with the way things are. Self-confident Christians are too busy to pray—they are confident that through their own hard work and sacrifice God's work will be done and His blessings will come. What, then, will bring us to our knees to seek God in prayer?

The first stage—a sense of crisis

God often awakens His people through times of crisis. That is what happened to Isaiah and caused him to seek God in the Temple (see Isaiah 6:1–8). That is what happened in the Moravian community. That is what happened before the Welsh revival. This has nearly always been the first stage in revivals of the past. Nearly always, some jolt or shock wakes Christians up to see their desperate need and causes them to seek God earnestly in prayer. Even when a crisis is man-made, God can use it to bring His greater purposes to pass.

The crisis may be because of an increase in lawlessness and fear in society. It may be the hopeless moral, political and spiritual depths to which our country has fallen. But the crisis may also be the spiritual decline and weakness of our churches. This should drive us as Christians to pray (though this doesn't always happen). God often brings His people to a point of desperation before He sends revival. For only then will we realize the truth of Jesus' words: "Apart from me you can do nothing" (John 15:5). Only then will we see the need to pray earnestly. Then as we begin to pray, God will begin to work.

The second stage—a burden to pray

When God sees that His people need revival, He lays a burden on their hearts to seek His face and pray. He may lay this on only a few.

God does many things in the world without the prayers of His people. But the amazing thing is, God will do some things only when His people are involved. And two areas where He waits for our involvement are *revival* and *evangelism.* God could sovereignly bring both of these to pass if He wanted to. However, for some reason He nearly always waits for our participation. He first lays a burden to pray upon the hearts of those who are open to Him. Then He brings His purposes to pass across the bridge of prayer (see 2 Chronicles 16:9). That's why persistent and passionate prayer has always come before every great move of God in the past. The first sign, then, of coming revival is usually a stirring up of the prayer life of God's people.

A Worldwide Prayer Movement

When we see God stirring up His people to pray, we can be sure He is about to do an amazing thing. And this is happening right now. Across the world Christians are feeling a burden to pray as never before. God is raising up a global prayer movement such as we have never seen before in the history of the world. Some have estimated as many as 170 million worldwide are involved in praying every day for spiritual awakening and world evangelization. In some places people have committed themselves to pray (and even to fast) around the clock in a continuous prayer chain.

Many Christians believe we are beginning to see revivals on a scale not seen before in the history of the Church. Each new day a wave of prayer is encircling the globe as believers of all nations and languages call on God to fulfill His purposes and send revival. God is up to something big, and He is calling you to be a part of what He is about to do (and has already begun)! Are you willing to be a part of it?

For Further Reflection

1. Read Luke 11:5–13.
2. Look again at the example of the Moravian revival at the start of the chapter. What impresses you most about this story of Nicholas von Zinzendorf?

3. God often uses times of crisis to bring His people to pray. What concerns are there about what is happening in society or in the Church? Are any of these concerns deep enough to cause God's people (and you) to pray desperately?

4. Think about Matthew Henry's quote at the start of the chapter. Why do you think God first gives His people a burden to pray before He sends revival? (See 2 Chronicles 7:14 and 16:9.)

5. A worldwide prayer movement: Reread the last section of the chapter. Are you willing to be a part of what God is doing in our time and to begin praying earnestly and regularly for revival? What is God saying to you through this chapter?

7

THE MARKS
OF REVIVAL PRAYING

*Every out-pouring of the Spirit is preceded by
earnest, agonizing intercession, accompanied by a
heart-brokenness and humiliation before God.*

Evan Roberts

If it be asked why the fire of God fell on Wales, the answer is
simple: Fire falls where it is likely to catch and spread. As one
has said, "Wales provided the necessary tinder." Here were
thousands of believers unknown to each other, in small towns
and villages and great cities, crying to God day after day for
the fire of God to fall. This was not merely a "little talk with
Jesus," but daily agonizing intercession. They had also placed
the wood upon the altar and had fully surrendered to the
claims of their Redeemer. They had a holy jealousy for the
name of their God and wept sorely because of the fact that
Satan was being glorified all around them. They constantly
reminded God of what He had done in the past: "O Lord, you
are the same," they cried, "and you can do it again—even in
this hurried, luxury-loving age." The Christians longed to see
a renewed manifestation of God's power. This was evident
in the earnestness of the weekly prayer-meetings and in the
conversation of God's people when they met together.

James Stewart, *Invasion of Wales by the Spirit*

When God lays a burden on the hearts of people to pray for revival, their praying is not ordinary praying. Pre-revival praying is not just an increase in personal prayer or an increase in the number of church prayer meetings. It is more than that. It is passionate praying. It is a shift of focus from just praying for personal needs to praying for God's greater purposes for His Church, for the city and for the nation. It is praying for the glory of God to come and the fire of God to fall. It is praying for the outpouring of His Holy Spirit. And it is praying that has a new intensity, urgency and passion. There are four main marks of revival praying.

Passionate Praying

Evan Roberts of the Welsh revival says:

> Every out-pouring of the Spirit is preceded by earnest, agonizing intercession, accompanied by a heart-brokenness and humiliation before God. . . . Deep spiritual awakenings, whether in local churches or in whole countries, begin with desperate people like Hannah. God only answers prayers of desperate Christians . . . Christians who are desperate about their own spiritual condition. While it is true that when the awakening does come there is "joy unspeakable and full of glory," this is not the case of the preparatory days. There is no song then, but rather groans; there is no laughter, but only tears.[1]

When God stirs His people to pray for revival, their prayers are marked with *fervor.* It is not that they deliberately turn away from formal prayers but simply that they cannot help it. It is as if their prayers catch alight with a new fire God has put within their hearts. Their prayers now burn with a passion and zeal for the glory and honor of God.

56

Revival praying is no longer driven by a sense of duty—it becomes the desire of the heart. Christians just can't help praying in private and together with other believers. And it is not just occasional praying but a constant and ongoing flow of intercession. And not just in a few scattered places but everywhere. Believers just want to pray. In Wales it began with a few praying, but gradually it built up until there were "thousands of believers unknown to each other, in small towns and villages and great cities, crying to God day after day for the fire of God to fall."[2] The fire did fall, but it came through the preparation of prayer. Just like a person starting a fire must first gather together many small twigs and sticks before striking a match, so the prayers of many believers whose hearts are seeking for God "provide the necessary tinder" for God's fire to catch alight.

Persistent Praying

The second mark of revival praying is *persistence.* God does not always answer our prayers for revival straightaway. Some people have carried the burden of revival praying for years before they have seen anything happen. Yet they did not give up—they kept on praying until God worked.

The whole Welsh revival began as a movement of prayer. Not only were there thousands of Christians in Wales praying for revival by 1904, but Evan Roberts had carried that prayer burden and prayed for revival for ten to eleven years before revival came. He would regularly wake at 1:00 A.M. and spend hours in communion with God. He said, "There was never a day when I didn't fling myself before God and cry out for Him to send the Holy Spirit to my native land."[3]

It is important to realize that this persistence in prayer was not always natural to those who prayed for revival—it was given to them by the Holy Spirit. It was said of Evan Roberts that when he was a boy, "he hardly ever saw anything through and would give up a task most easily."[4] But now the Holy Spirit had put a burden in his heart for revival so that his praying was passionate and persistent.

Today we may pray for revival occasionally, but not persistently. We may pray casually, but not urgently. We may easily turn aside to more immediate and personal concerns. This does not mean that we should not also pray for other things, but if we are to see revival, some Christians, somewhere, must pray continually and persistently until the outpouring of the Holy Spirit comes.

Persuasive Praying

The third mark of revival praying is praying with *persuasion*. This does not mean we try to change God's mind or convince Him of our need. Persuasive praying simply means taking the promises of God concerning what He desires to do and praying them back to Him: "Lord, this is what You have said You will do, so bring it to pass." Those who pray for revival plead the clear promises of a covenant-keeping God by praying according to the truths of Scripture. They stretch their prayers to the width of God's promises and wait on God to do what He has said He will do. God has said that in the last days He will pour out His Spirit upon all people. He has said that times of refreshing will come from the presence of the Lord. He has said that He will make His Bride (the Church) radiant and ready for His coming. We hold on to these promises and keep praying them back to Him until they are fulfilled.

Penitent Praying

The fourth mark of revival praying is a *deep sorrow over sin. Penitent* speaks of a humble, contrite and repentant heart. This sorrow over sin is not just for personal sin (though it will include that) but also sorrow for the sins of the Church and the nation.

As we look at the prayers of godly people in Old Testament times, we see that whenever they approached God with a plea for revival, they nearly always began by acknowledging their own sin and the sins of their people (see Nehemiah 1:4–9). The same has been true throughout history. Nearly every revival contains the record of people coming to God with penitent prayers before the revival started—openly confessing their sins and the sins of their people. Where sin stands in the way of God's blessings, this must first be dealt with. Prayers of confession and repentance must be offered before God can move in power. This often has to be done on behalf of God's people or a nation (what we call *identificational repentance*), which requires a deep humbling of oneself. And that's why God responds (see Proverbs 3:34). How often have you experienced this humbling sense of penitence in your own prayers, and how often have you seen it in prayer meetings you have attended?

God is looking for those who will pray down revival. Are you willing to say yes to Him by humbly coming before Him in prayer? God waits for His people to humble themselves and pray before He moves in power and blessing.

For Further Reflection

1. Read Acts 4:23–31. What were the marks of this prayer meeting?
2. How were believers across Wales praying before the revival of 1904? What were the marks of their praying?
3. Look again at the example of the prayer life of Evan Roberts before revival came. How does his prayer life speak to you personally?
4. Persuasive praying: What are some of God's promises of what He will do? (See Isaiah 44:3–5; Acts 2:17; Ephesians

5:25–27.) Pause right now and pray some of these promises back to Him.

5. Penitent praying: As you look at the prayers of godly people in Old Testament times, what do you notice about the way they prayed? (See Nehemiah 1:4–9; Jeremiah 14:19–21; Daniel 9:4–11.) What can you learn from their example?

6. Are you willing to make yourself available for God to put this burden for revival on your heart? Ask Him to do that. Then make a commitment this week to begin praying for revival.

PART 4

INTIMACY
WITH GOD

Second Chronicles 7:14, as I have already mentioned, tells us the conditions of God's favor and blessing. We have looked at the first two conditions—humbling ourselves and praying. Now we come to the *third condition* of revival:

If my people, who are called by my name, will

- humble themselves (brokenness)
- pray (dependence)
- *seek my face (intimacy)*
- turn from their wicked ways (repentance)

61

Then will I

- hear from heaven
- forgive their sin
- heal their land

God calls us not only to pray but to *seek His face.* What does this mean? Seeking God's face brings us to the heart of what revival is all about. It moves us into a deeper dimension of prayer and fellowship with God. In the next three chapters we will look at what this means.

8

Seeking God's Face

If you want revival, don't seek for revival—seek Him. To enter into a deep and intimate relationship with Jesus is revival.

Michael Maeliau

The third condition of revival in 2 Chronicles 7:14 is *seeking God's face*. But what does this mean? Seeking God's face is the very heart of what revival is all about. It is a deeper dimension of prayer. It speaks of closeness, fellowship, openness and intimacy with God. It brings us into the realm of praise, adoration, worship, enjoying God's presence, listening to His voice, responding to His love. It is more than just seeking God for what He can do; it is seeking God for who He is. It is more than just seeking His blessings; it is seeking God for Himself alone.

Jesus Is Revival

In seeking revival we can make the mistake of seeking the signs, the experiences and the blessings that may come with revival but failing to seek Jesus! But Jesus *is* revival. Revival is the result or by-product of seeking and knowing Jesus more intimately. So it is not even revival that we should seek first of all but a fresh love and passion for Jesus. To enter into deep and intimate fellowship with Jesus *is* revival!

63

We can give ourselves to prayer but still fail to *seek God's face.* We can think that prayer is just praying for requests—seeking God for His gifts, for healing, for His blessings, for our needs, for our ministry and even for revival itself. But in all this we can miss out on the most important thing of all. God desires that we seek not just His hand (what He can do for us) but that we seek His face. Our highest priority and greatest privilege is fellowship and intimacy with God. God wants you above everything else to seek *Him.*

Longing for Intimacy

One of the most amazing truths of Scripture is that God desires your fellowship. He searches for you. He calls you by name. He invites you to come. He longs that you know Him intimately. And He has done everything possible to open the way into His presence. But what is your response? Will you draw near, or will you stay at a distance?

As we look in the pages of Scripture, we see ordinary people who drew near to God like this—people like Enoch, Abraham, Moses, David, Paul and others. These people had a passion for God's presence and a longing to know Him more. They responded to God's call and sought Him with all their hearts. This opened the door to intimacy with God. Jonathan Edwards, who was used mightily in the First Great Awakening in America (1734–80), said that it is through intimacy with heaven that we are made great blessings on earth. God has no favorites—He desires all His children to know Him in this deep way. And that includes you!

Living under God's Favor

We can know God intimately only if we are living under His favor. In the Old Testament, God's feelings toward us are described using the human terms of His *face.* If He turns His face toward us, smiles or shines His face upon us, this means God is pleased with us and we are living under His favor. The result of this is wholeness, strength, grace, peace, joy and purpose—in other words, knowing God's blessing. But if God turns or hides His face from us, this means He is displeased, angry or grieved, and we are living without God's favor and without His blessing. This results in loss of joy, loss of purpose and emptiness.

Is God pleased with me? Is His face turned toward me? Am I living under His favor, or am I not? These are the most important questions of life. My whole life and future depend on the answer. Yet there is no doubt about what God desires. He longs to shine His face upon you and be gracious to you. He wants to bless you. He rises to show you compassion. He delights to fill your life with good things. But this all depends on your response to Him. Do you long for His favor? Do you desire to seek His face? You can only "seek God's face" if His face is turned toward you. Psalm 80:3 tells us that when God shines His face upon us, that *is* revival!

Three Requirements for Seeking His Face

A longing to know God

First, you must have a desire to know God intimately. David said:

> Your face, LORD, I will seek.
> Do not hide your face from me.
>
> Psalm 27:8–9

It is possible, sadly, to know about God—to have information, knowledge and facts about Him—but not to know Him personally and intimately. But He desires that you *know* Him.

65

The word in Scripture for "knowing" God is the same word used for the most intimate personal relationship between a husband and wife. This is what God has made us for—that we might have a deep, intimate love relationship with the Father, Son and Spirit that grows sweeter and deeper throughout the passing years. This will find its complete fulfillment in the heavenly wedding ceremony, when we are united with Christ forever (see Revelation 19:7–9). Is this what you are longing for?

Taking time to seek Him

Second, as in any relationship, if you want to develop a close relationship with a person, you need to spend quality time together and express by words and actions your love for each other. This is also true of your relationship with God. Intimacy with God can only come from taking time to be alone with Him. But this is not just to present your requests to Him (though this has its place). Intimacy comes from *seeking His face*—taking time to worship, expressing to Him your love and adoration, bringing your whole life before Him and responding to His love. Do you take time each day to do that?

Dealing with obstacles

Third, as is true in any human relationship, intimacy can develop only when problems in the relationship are dealt with and removed. Are things in your life causing Him to hide His face from you, grieving His Spirit and so preventing you from experiencing Him closely? Psalm 24:3–6 tells us what is required of those who would seek God and draw near to Him in His holy place. It gives us a checklist of the kinds of things we must watch out for if we would be a part of "the generation of those who seek Him." God delights to bless and honor those who seek Him like this. Are you going to be one of them?

For Further Reflection

1. Read Psalm 27:4–9; Hebrews 10:19–22.
2. What do you think it means to *seek God's face?* In what ways is this more than just "praying"?
3. What is our greatest privilege and the most important thing of all according to Psalms 27:4, 8; 46:10; 105:3–4? What do these references say to you?
4. What does the description of "God's face" mean in the following references? Numbers 6:24–26; Deuteronomy 31:17; Psalm 44:3. What does God long to do for you? (See Isaiah 30:18.)
5. What was the deepest longing in the hearts of Moses and Paul? (See Exodus 33:11; Philippians 3:8–10.) What is your deepest longing?
6. Three requirements for seeking His face: Look again at this section. What has God been saying to you about each of these areas?
7. If you do not already set aside time each day to read God's Word, pray and seek His face, then begin doing so. Set aside at least fifteen to twenty minutes. Read and meditate daily on one of the following Bible passages, and use the thoughts from these passages to guide you into thanksgiving, praise and worship: Psalms 8; 24; 27:1–14; 63; 84; 103.

9

SUBSTITUTES FOR INTIMACY

*Work for Christ has sometimes drawn away from
Christ and taken the place of fellowship with Him.*

Andrew Murray, *Abiding in Christ*

God longs that we know Him intimately. Yet it is easier
to settle for something less than a close relationship
with Jesus. We can be content to know *about* Him rather than
to *know* Him. We can even be busy serving Him but miss out
on the joy of fellowship with Him. Three main things can take
the place of intimacy with God.

"Religion" Rather than Relationship

Some Christians have settled for a form of godliness based
on rules, routines and traditions, rather than relationship. They
think the meaning of Christianity is simply going to church,
reading the Bible and saying prayers rather than seeking God's
face. They may "know" God with their minds but do not really
know Him intimately as He desires to be known.

The heart of Christianity is neither law nor religious duty
but a love relationship with Jesus. Those who settle for rules
and rituals instead of intimacy have a form of godliness but

do not know the presence or the power of God. Jesus said of the religious people of His day:

> These people honor me with their lips,
> but their hearts are far from me.
>
> Matthew 15:8–9

Right words, but wrong heart! Right actions, but no relationship!

Relying on religious routine

Wayne Jacobsen says, "Religious routine is the first thing we grab when the freshness of God's presence dries up."[1] When spiritually dry times come and our prayers and Bible reading become empty, we are faced with a choice—we can either fall back on religious routine and continue to do what we have done before but try a little harder; or else we can come before God to find out why the spring has dried up and how to have His presence restored. The solution is to seek God's face more earnestly. But this means finding out what He wants to change in us. And something in all of us would rather fall back into the comfort of religious ritual than risk the personal sacrifice and change God might ask of us.

Don't become a Pharisee!

If we continue to maintain an outward form of godliness with no heart relationship, we will soon become like the Pharisees of Jesus' day. But religious ritual with no relationship is what God hates (see Amos 5:21–24)! Jesus strongly condemned this hollow Pharisee attitude (see Matthew 23:25–28). The heart of Christianity is not rules but relationship—being deeply in love with Jesus. What God desires above all else is that you know and love Him with all your heart (see Matthew 22:37–38).

69

A Mediator Rather than a Personal Meeting with God

The second way we can miss out on intimacy with God is to let other people go to God for us instead of seeking God ourselves. This is what the Israelites did. When God came down to meet with them on Mount Sinai, instead of drawing near to hear God for themselves, they asked Moses to stand before God for them and then to tell them what to do (see Exodus 20:18–21). On this point Richard Foster says:

> The history of religion is the story of an almost desperate scramble to have a king, a mediator, a priest, a go-between. In this way we do not need to go to God ourselves. Such an approach saves us from the need to change, for to be in the presence of God is to change. It is very convenient this way because it gives us the advantage of religious respectability without demanding moral transformation.[2]

The desire for a human mediator

The fire of God's presence burns away sin, confronts our self-life and unmasks our complacency. This can be painful, costly and humbling. Little wonder it is something we naturally want to avoid! It is easier to depend on someone else—a minister, your pastor, well-known speakers, even Christian books or tapes—and let them speak God's message to you, rather than seeking God's face for yourself. Or you may rely on the spiritual life of your wife or husband, a friend, a counselor, your parents or some other spiritually mature Christian, rather than seeking God personally. Let them listen to God and find out what He wants, and you will do as they say. Let the pastor spend time with God in prayer and give God's message each week, and you will be content with that. But is that what you want—secondhand Christianity? Would you rather stay at a distance (like the Israelites) than draw near and know God yourself?

70

Draw near to God yourself

Scripture makes it clear that every believer has the right to come into God's presence (see Hebrews 10:19–22). In fact, God invites you to come. You can know Him intimately. You can hear Him speak personally. That is why God calls you to draw near to Him constantly. Do not send someone else! Enter His presence yourself, for He wants to meet with you personally. If you remain at a distance and rely on a human mediator, you are missing out on the joy of intimacy, and your Christian life will remain shallow and weak as a result. Is that what you want? "Come near to God, and he will come near to you" (James 4:8).

Busyness

Busyness is the third thing that can keep you from intimacy with God and lead to spiritual barrenness. Intimacy with God requires a quiet, focused life. Quietness is needed when you cease for a time from busyness and activity and seek God in stillness and solitude. You cannot enter meaningfully into prayer, worship, meditation and listening for His voice in the midst of noise, busyness and hurry. And focus is required, for there will always be other things that call for your time and attention. Therefore, you must make time alone with God the first priority of your life. It must be the source from which everything else flows—just as it was for Jesus (see Mark 1:35).

The story of Mary and Martha shows us clearly that while there is a time to be busy, there is also a time to sit quietly at the Master's feet in worship, adoration and fellowship with Him. This is what Jesus wants more than anything else. It must come even before our desire to serve Him. While Jesus accepted Martha's desire to serve, He reminded her that what He wanted most of all was what Mary had chosen—not her service but *herself.* Maybe that's what He wants of you too!

We can easily fall into the trap of seeing our busyness in Christian service as a good reason for not having time to sit quietly at Jesus' feet. But if we are that busy serving God, we are busier than God intends and are doing (like Martha) more than He requires of us. Service must never become a substitute for intimacy. Work must never take the place of worship.

For Further Reflection

1. Read Exodus 20:18–21; Luke 10:38–42.
2. Religion rather than relationship: What kind of things does God hate, according to Amos 5:21–24 and Matthew 15:8–9? Why does God hate these things? What is wrong with this kind of Christianity?
3. What do you think God is saying to you about this first substitute for intimacy (religion versus relationship)? How can you tell if you have become "religious" rather than intimate (see Matthew 22:37–38)?
4. A mediator rather than meeting God personally: Reread the quotation by Richard Foster in the second point of the chapter. Do you think even as Christians we can tend to rely on mediators rather than seeking God for ourselves? In what ways?
5. Rather than relying on others to meet God for us, what does God desire? (See Psalm 27:8; Hebrews 10:19–22.)
6. Busyness: What important lessons can you see in this story of Mary and Martha? (See Luke 10:38–42.) How do they apply to you? If Jesus were to come and speak to you right now, what do you think He might say to you?

10

STEPS TO INTIMACY WITH GOD

*Intimacy with God is found in a quiet and focused
life. Hurriedness and clamor drive out his presence.*

Wayne Jacobsen, *A Passion for God's Presence*

Many things can keep us from intimacy with God. In the last chapter we looked at three such hindrances. But how can we enjoy intimacy with God? There are several important steps.

Understand That God Longs for You

In Psalm 27:8 (RSV) God says, "Seek my face." And in Revelation 3:20 the living Lord says to the church at Laodicea, "Here I am! I stand at the door and knock." Both verses express the longing in the heart of God for fellowship with us. He longs that we come to Him and meet with Him face-to-face. He longs that we as His people open the door into our hearts and into our church assemblies so that He might come and fellowship with us. How often have we gone ahead with our worship and church activities and not even realized He was not there? When God said to David, "Seek my face," David's response was clear: "Your face, LORD, I will seek" (Psalm 27:8). Are you willing to seek His face like David did? This is the first step. He is longing for you to come.

Take Time to Be Alone with God

The second step toward intimacy with God is responding to His desire to meet with you. Take time each day to be alone with Him. Make it a daily practice. It has always been the mark of those who have walked close with God that they have spent time alone with Him each day. David did (see Psalm 5:3). Daniel did (see Daniel 6:10). Even Jesus, who had no sin, took time to be alone with His Father (see Mark 1:35). How much more, then, should we! Ask God to put in your heart a longing to seek Him in a way you have never sought Him before.

> As the deer pants for streams of water,
> so my soul pants for you, O God.
>
> Psalm 42:1

Learn to Listen for His Voice

Third, understand that prayer is more than asking for things. Prayer is, above everything else, communion with God—receiving His love, enjoying His presence, bowing in adoration and worship and listening to what He wants to say to you. Mary sat at Jesus' feet listening to what He said (see Luke 10:39). How often in prayer do you do all the talking and very little listening? Prayer in its simplest form is just entering into an attitude of saying, "Lord, what do You want to say to me?"

Our relationship with God will never grow deep if we do not learn to listen and respond to what He says. We would miss out on so many things He wants to share with us. Intimacy grows out of sharing what is upon your heart and also listening to what is upon God's heart. Listen as you read His Word. Listen as you wait quietly in His presence. Say what Samuel said: "Speak, LORD, for your servant is listening" (1 Samuel 3:9). Then try to listen for His voice. It may be a thought that drops into your mind or a mental picture or vision that comes to you. It may be a holy desire that rises in your heart or an inner prompting or conviction that challenges you to some action. God can speak in many ways—learn to recognize His voice. Jesus said, "My sheep listen to my voice . . . and they follow me" (John 10:27). Are you listening? Are you following?

Become a Worshiper

Fourth, intimacy with God grows deeper as you take time to worship. Mary was a worshiper. She expressed her love and devotion by pouring out on Jesus precious perfume (see John 12:1–8). When you come into God's presence, be a worshiper first. Pour out on Jesus your love and devotion. Take time to express to Him the awe you feel when you recognize who He is and what He has done for you. Speak words of gratitude and praise for His greatness, power, mercy, forgiveness and love for you. Be generous (like Mary), not mean and calculating (like the disciples). Give Him your best. Give Him your all. Worship is like pouring out sweet perfume upon Jesus' head and feet. Not only does this honor Him, but it deepens your love for Him. It also fills your life with the sweet fragrance of His presence that will touch others around you.

Share the Deep Levels of Your Life with Him

This is the fifth step toward intimacy. Just spending time with a person does not guarantee intimacy—the level at which you share will determine how deep your relationship becomes. Intimacy comes out of sharing from your heart. It is sharing with a person not just what you think but who you really are and what you feel deep within. Many Christians suppose that in prayer they must only think and express spiritual thoughts, that they must keep their fears, failures, hurts, anger, resentment, unholy thoughts and sinful attitudes hidden from God's presence. But prayer means to bring all you are into the presence of God. He knows everything about you anyway! Intimacy will only develop when you are willing to open your heart to God and say, "Lord, this is what I am. This is how I feel. This is what I'm struggling with. I'm angry with that person. I can't release that hurt. I don't want to forgive. I have these wrong thoughts and attitudes," or whatever you need to say. As long as you keep these deep areas of your life hidden from God, He cannot deal with them. But when you bring them into the light as He is in the light, He will heal, forgive, cleanse and restore. And He will change your heart and deepen your fellowship with Him and with others.

Be Obedient to What He Says

Intimacy with God grows as we respond to His prompting and obey His commands. Jesus said, "You are my friends if you do what I command" (John 15:14). Abraham was called *a friend of God* (James 2:23) not only because he listened to God's voice but also because he obeyed whatever God commanded him. Are you obeying God in everything He has revealed to you? Friendship and intimacy with God are reserved for those who love and obey Him. "If anyone loves me," Jesus said, "he will obey my teaching. My Father will love him, and we will come to him and make our home with him" (John 14:23).

Live a Holy Life

God is holy. He is pure and separate from sin. If we are to draw near to Him, therefore, we must be holy also. Holiness means being separated from sin and being set apart for sacred use. It is living the way God wants me to live. It is offering every part of my life to Him. It is always doing those things that please Him. Holiness is never a result of self-effort in observing laws or trying our best to measure up to certain standards. It comes simply as a result of surrendering to the Spirit of Christ who lives within. For the Holy Spirit is "the Spirit of holiness" (Romans 1:4). He alone can make me holy. He alone can make me like Christ. He alone can bring me near to God (see Ephesians 2:18). And to be holy is simply to be like Jesus. This is why, when the Holy Spirit comes in revival, He always brings conviction of sin first and then a revival of holiness. This is so we might be brought back into the light where we can have fellowship again with our Father who loves us. Is that what you want? Then begin to take the seven steps toward God that we have looked at in this chapter.

For Further Reflection

1. Read John 12:1–8.
2. Understand that God longs for you: In Psalm 27:8 (RSV) God says, "Seek my face." And in Revelation 3:20 the living Lord says to a church, "Here I am! I stand at the door and knock." What do these verses tell us God desires? What is your response?
3. Take time to be alone with God: What was a clear priority and constant practice of the following people— David (see Psalm 5:3), Daniel (see Daniel 6:10), Jesus (see Mark 1:35)? And what did Jesus tell His disciples to do as a regular practice? (See Matthew 6:6.) What is God saying to you about this area of your relationship with Him?
4. Learn to listen for His voice: As Mary took time to sit at Jesus' feet, what was she mainly doing? (See Luke 10:39.) Think about your own prayer life. How often do you take

time to listen (as Mary did)? What is God saying to you about this part of your prayer life? (See John 10:27.)

5. Become a worshiper: What do you think Mary's act of pouring out costly perfume on Jesus did to her relationship with Him? (See Matthew 26:6–13 and John 12:1–3.) What will expressing your love and devotion do to your relationship with Jesus?

6. Share the deep levels of your life with Him: Reread the fifth point in the chapter. What happens when we are willing to be honest and bring all we are (bad as well as good) into the light of God's presence? (See 1 John 1:6–9.) Do you do this?

THE ESSENTIAL KEY— REPENTANCE

We have looked at the first three conditions of revival—humbling ourselves, praying and seeking God's face. In Part 5 we look at the *fourth condition* mentioned in 2 Chronicles 7:14:

If my people, who are called by my name, will

- humble themselves (brokenness)
- pray (dependence)
- seek my face (intimacy)
- *turn from their wicked ways (repentance)*

Then will I

- hear from heaven
- forgive their sin
- heal their land

At first it seems that the order of the conditions of revival in 2 Chronicles 7:14 is wrong. Shouldn't we "turn from our wicked ways" first before we "pray and seek God's face"? Shouldn't there be repentance before we can seek fellowship and intimacy with God?

The truth is simply this: We do not know what to repent of until God reveals our true condition. While we are living in the shadows, we cannot see what we are really like and do not know that repentance is needed. But when we come to the light in prayer and in seeking God's face, we become aware of things not right within and see things as they really are (see Isaiah 6:1–8). Only in the light of God's holiness will we be able to come to true repentance.

11

WHERE REVIVAL BEGINS

Revivals do not begin happily with everyone having a good time. They start with a broken and contrite heart.

Peterus Octavianus

In 1907 there was a powerful move of God in North Korea. This is how a Western missionary described one meeting:

As the prayer continued, a spirit of heaviness and sorrow for sin came down upon the audience. Over on one side, someone began to weep, and in a moment the whole audience was weeping. One person after another would rise, confess his sins, break down and weep, and then throw himself to the floor and beat the floor with his fists in perfect agony of conviction. . . . Sometimes after a confession, the whole audience would break out in audible prayer, and the effect of that audience of hundreds of people praying together in audible prayer was something indescribable. Again, after another confession, they would break out in uncontrollable weeping, and we would all weep, we could not help it. And so the meeting went on until two o'clock in the morning, with confession and weeping and praying. . . . Some threw themselves full length on the floor, hundreds stood with arms outstretched toward heaven. Every person forgot every other. Each was face to face with God. I can still hear that fearful sound of hundreds of people pleading with God for life, for mercy.[1]

Scenes like this are typical of almost every recorded revival. I can recall vividly a very similar spirit of conviction falling on a meeting in the Solomon Islands during an Easter convention after a message on the holiness of God. This was but a preparation for an even greater visitation and infilling that took place on the last day of that convention. (See Postscript on page 189.)

Often we have a one-sided view of revival as a time of glory and joy with people flooding into our churches. This is only part of the story. Before the glory and joy, there must come conviction, and that begins with the people of God. Conviction is always one of the primary works of the Holy Spirit (see John 16:8). It is a necessary preparation for His renewing and infilling. He cannot fill us until we are clean.

He will make us see things in our lives and in our churches that are grieving and hindering His working. When He shines His divine searchlight into our hearts, it may cause great pain and agony of spirit as we see ourselves as we really are. There will be tears and godly sorrow. There will come an awareness of wrongs that must be put right, secret sins that must be confessed and dealt with, broken relationships that must be repaired.

Without this convicting work we can never be revived, and God's purposes will continue to be hindered in us and in His Church. This is why deep conviction of sin is such a constant feature of all true revivals. Revival is not intended to make us happy but to make us holy. And there can be no revival without this deep, uncomfortable and often humbling conviction of sin that leads to repentance.

What Is Repentance?

Repentance is more than regret or remorse. It is more than just being sorry, or apologizing to God. Repentance is deep conviction that brings a change of heart and leads to a change of behavior (reformation). A temporary change of behavior is not enough—it must be a permanent change if it is true repentance. Repentance is recognizing we are living and behaving in a way that grieves God's Spirit and then turning and changing to live the way God wants us to live.

Repentance is an ongoing process

Some think that repentance has only to do with conversion. But it is more than that. Our whole Christian life must be one of ongoing repentance if we are to walk in the light with Jesus. God will continue to reveal things in our lives we must deal with and forsake—deeper and deeper levels of ingrained sin He wants to purge from us so that we may grow in holiness. We see this happening in the seven churches of Asia Minor. The living Lord called five of these seven churches to repent (see Revelation 2:5, 16, 22; 3:3, 19). If He called these Christians to repent of wrong things in their lives, what would the living Lord say to us today?

Repentance is a gift from God

True repentance can only come as a convicting work of the Holy Spirit (see John 16:8). That is why conviction falls so strongly on people in times of revival. Without the Spirit's convicting work, we will never see our sin nor feel its pain and, therefore, will not feel the need to do anything about it. But God in His mercy reaches out to us. It is through His Spirit that He brings conviction of sin and brings us to repentance. He strips away our disguises and excuses. He lays bare our self-deception. He reveals the depth of our self-life. He deals with all that is unholy in our lives. We could not come to repentance on our own. True repentance is always a gift from God (see Acts 11:17–18; Romans 2:4).

Repentance is a response to revelation

True repentance does not come by gazing inward and trying to find things wrong in our lives. This only leads to misery, self-condemnation and loss of joy and may result in shallow repentance and self-forgiveness. True repentance comes as we look upward and see God in His holiness. It comes in response to God's revelation of Himself and then a revelation of ourselves. When we see God more clearly in His holiness, we see ourselves more clearly in our sinfulness. The more we seek God and move toward the light, the more we will become conscious of wrongs within that need to be dealt with. Then the Holy Spirit leads us to repentance and then to cleansing, release and revival. But how will we know what to repent of until God reveals our true condition? (See 1 John 1:7–9.)

No Repentance, No Revival

In times of revival, when God's Spirit is moving powerfully, people are often overcome with deep grief over things that in normal times seem small and unimportant. But that is what God's presence does. It shows things as they really are. Revival will not come any way; it will come only God's way. And without repentance, there will be no revival.

A. W. Tozer said that there can be "no revival without reformation." Repentance means a change of heart, which must lead to a change of behavior (reformation). Both must go together if we are to "turn from our wicked ways." Tozer goes on to say:

> Unless we intend to reform, we may as well not pray. Unless praying men have the insight and faith to amend their whole way of life to conform to the New Testament pattern, there can be no true revival.
>
> We must have a reformation within the church. To beg for a flood of blessing to come upon a backslidden and disobedient church is to waste time and effort. A new wave of religious interest will do no more than add numbers to the churches that have no intention to own the Lordship of Jesus and come under obedience to his commandments. God is not

interested in increasing church attendance unless those who attend amend their ways and begin to live holy lives.

Prayer for revival will prevail when it is accompanied by radical amendment of life; not before. All night prayer meetings that are not preceded by practical repentance may actually be displeasing to God. "To obey is better than sacrifice" (1 Samuel 15:22).[2]

Repentance, therefore, is the key to revival for it is both a preparation for revival and an ongoing part of revival. If repentance dies, so does revival. We cannot continue to experience revival without it. God cannot bless His people with revival if there is an unwillingness to repent and to change, for the very reason we need revival is that there are things in our lives that need to be dealt with. Someone at the time of the revival in Borneo in 1973 said that what the Church in Borneo needed most of all was "not an increase of bright gatherings or an emotional high, but repentance, confession and the forsaking of sin."[3] What was true of the Church in Borneo before revival is true of our churches today. What we need most of all is repentance, confession and the forsaking of sin. That is the key that opens the door to revival.

What Leads Us to Repentance?

According to Richard Lovelace, the two main things that lead to repentance and revival are, first, an awareness of the *holiness of God,* and second, an awareness of the *depth of sin.*[4] Preaching on these areas can prepare the way, but it must be Holy Spirit–anointed preaching. If it is not, it will lead people to condemnation only, rather than to conviction. But anointed proclamation of the Word of God is what the Spirit uses to bring revelation, conviction of sin and repentance. A shallow understanding of who God is and what He requires will lead

85

to shallow repentance. But a deep awareness of God's holiness and our sin will lead to deep repentance.

Proclamation of God's Word

In the Old Testament stories of revival, the clear proclamation of the Word of God began the whole process. We see this in the revivals under Josiah, Nehemiah and Jonah. In the revival under Nehemiah, Ezra began reading the words of the Law to the gathered assembly from dawn until noon. As the words were expounded and explained, the people responded with awe and worship and came under such deep conviction that they wept and mourned uncontrollably at the fresh awareness of the depth of their sin (see Nehemiah 8). This was the start of reformation and revival (see Nehemiah 9).

At the time of the Protestant Reformation in Europe (1517), Martin Luther's study of the Scriptures brought him to see the depth of his own sin and his need of spiritual renewal. It also brought him to realize that crucial truths of Scripture had been lost in the teaching of the Church and must be reclaimed and reapplied. This in turn stirred him to preach with great conviction and led to the start of the Protestant Reformation.

Revelation of God's holiness

At the time of the First Spiritual Awakening in America (in the 1730s), the Puritans and Pietists (such as Jonathan Edwards) had a fresh revelation of God's holiness and human sinfulness that led them to preach passionately on these themes. This resulted in the start of the First Great Awakening. It was said at the time that one of the prominent features of the Great Awakening was that "the Gospel was armed by the Holy Spirit with a tremendous and irresistible *individualizing* power."[5] Man was made to come forth into the light and take his stand before God as guilty and accountable. The preachers knew that the absence of godly fear was ruining people from one generation to the next. They also knew that even the truth preached with great conviction could not by itself induce the fear that leads to repentance and eternal life. Only a *consciousness* of the presence of God could make the truths preached startlingly real and compelling to both preachers and hearers alike.

In every true revival in history this same process is seen— first, a fresh revelation of God through anointed proclamation of the Word, which in turn brings awareness of the holiness of God followed by conviction, open confession of sin and repentance. Jonathan Goforth of China said, "We can entertain no hope of a mighty, globe-encircling Holy Spirit revival without there being first a back-to-the-Bible movement."[6] If we are to see revival today in our churches, the same will be true for us. There can be no revival without a fresh awareness of the holiness of God, the depth of sin and a deep and lasting turning back to God in repentance.

For Further Reflection

1. Read Acts 2:36–41; 11:15–18.
2. "I don't need to repent," a church member said angrily. "I repented when I became a Christian, and that's all that is needed!" Is this a right understanding of repentance? What else is needed? (See 1 John 1:8–10.)
3. What did the living Lord call five of the seven churches of Asia Minor to do? (See Revelation 2:4–5, 15–16, 20–22; 3:1–3, 15–20.) Why was this necessary? Do you think this still applies to our churches today (and to your life personally)?
4. Look again at the quotation by A. W. Tozer in the chapter. According to Tozer, why is repentance and reformation necessary before there can be revival?
5. Look again at the story from North Korea at the start of the chapter. Why do you think conviction fell upon the people like this? What does all this mean?

6. Think about the revival under Ezra (see Nehemiah 8:1–12; 9:1–3) and the First Spiritual Awakening in America. What two main things lead to repentance and revival? Why are both needed together?

7. Do you think Christians today have a clear awareness of the holiness of God and the depth of sin? What view does the average Christian in your church have? What about you? What is God saying to you through this study?

12

INDIVIDUAL REPENTANCE

General confession of sin will never do. Your sins were committed one by one, and they should be reviewed and repented of one by one.

Charles Finney, *Revivals of Religion*

There are three levels of repentance. The first is *individual repentance,* the second *corporate repentance* (as a church) and the third *identificational repentance* (on behalf of others). In this chapter we will look at the first of these.

We Must Repent as Individuals

Psalm 24 tells us what is required of those who would seek God and draw near to Him in His holy place. It gives us a checklist of the kinds of things we must watch out for if we would be a part of the generation of those who seek Him (verse 6). The marks of those who would seek God's face are "clean hands" (holy actions), "a pure heart" (holy attitudes), no idolatry (holy affections) and no falsehood (holy words). But what causes God to hide His face from us? The opposite of these things—wrong actions, wrong attitudes, idolatry and falsehood. We must recognize and turn away from these things.

Charles Finney was a revival preacher in the nineteenth century (1825–1860). He prepared a list of possible sins for people to check their lives against, as he believed it was no use just talking about sin in a general way—we may easily excuse ourselves. Repentance must be specific. Specific sins must be listed, therefore, so that we can judge our lives more accurately. With this in mind, carefully work through the lists below and ask God to reveal to you any of the things that may be affecting your life (even in the smallest way). Be honest!

Wrong actions (unclean hands?)

☐ Lack of integrity with finances

☐ Dishonest/wrong practices

☐ Taking what is not yours

☐ Not doing your work well

☐ Careless, lazy

☐ Neglect of your family

☐ Inflicting physical or emotional hurt

☐ Unfair treatment of others

☐ Dishonoring your parents

☐ Bad temper

☐ Compulsive or secret habits

☐ Living in an immoral relationship

☐ Wrong sexual activities

Wrong attitudes (an impure heart?)

☐ Unbelief

☐ Independent and rebellious spirit

☐ Critical of others

☐ Resentful

☐ Hard to get along with

☐ Unforgiving

☐ Self-centered

☐ Demanding

☐ Selfish

☐ Little concern for needs of others

☐ Little concern for unsaved

☐ Proud spirit

☐ Envious or jealous of others

☐ Ungrateful

☐ Complaining

☐ Unwilling to confess or apologize

Wrong affections (idolatry?)

- ☐ Impure thoughts
- ☐ Sexual fantasies or imaginations
- ☐ Reading/watching immoral books/movies
- ☐ Viewing pornographic materials
- ☐ Love of money and material possessions
- ☐ Desire for wealth—lotteries, gambling
- ☐ Tight and controlling
- ☐ Lacking a generous, giving spirit
- ☐ Self-centered interests
- ☐ Little hunger for God
- ☐ Little time alone with God
- ☐ Putting another person before God
- ☐ Putting work (business) before God
- ☐ Putting sports (interests) before God
- ☐ Robbing God of time
- ☐ Robbing God of money (not tithing)
- ☐ Neglect of prayer and God's Word
- ☐ Neglect of Christian fellowship
- ☐ Trusting in lucky charms, horoscope
- ☐ Life controlled by financial concerns
- ☐ Little love or passion for Jesus

Wrong words (falsehood?)

- ☐ Tendency to lie or exaggerate
- ☐ Putting others down
- ☐ Talking against others
- ☐ Critical of others
- ☐ Tendency to gossip/slander
- ☐ Using verbal abuse
- ☐ Swearing
- ☐ Unkind or harsh words
- ☐ Untrue words
- ☐ Promises not kept

Dealing with these sins

Following Charles Finney's list of possible sins, he then gave the following instructions:

As you go over the list of your sins, be sure to decide upon immediate and entire reformation. Wherever you find anything wrong, commit yourself at once in the strength of God, to sin no more in that way. It will be of no benefit to examine yourself, unless you determine to change, in every respect, that which you find wrong in heart, temper or conduct.

Go now! Do not put it off! That will only make matters worse. Confess to God those sins that have been committed against God, and to man, those sins that have been committed against man.

Things may be left that you may think are little things and you may wonder why you don't have peace with God, when the reason is your proud and carnal mind has covered up something which God requires you to confess and remove.

Unless you take up your sins in this way and consider them in detail, one by one, you can form no idea of the amount or weight of them. You should go over the list as thoroughly and as carefully and as solemnly as if you were preparing yourself for the judgement![1]

The four essentials

In the Welsh revival of 1904, Evan Roberts continually set before people what became known as "the four points." He would ask the people if they really wanted an outpouring of the Spirit of God. Then he would give them these four conditions that he believed were essential:

Is there any sin in your past that you have not confessed to God? On your knees at once! Your past must be put away and your self cleansed.

Is there anything in your life that is doubtful—anything that you cannot decide whether it is good or evil? Away with it! There must not be a cloud between you and God. Have you forgiven everybody, EVERYBODY? If not, don't expect forgiveness for your own sins. You won't get it!

Do what the Spirit prompts you to do. Obedience—prompt, implicit, unquestioning obedience to the Spirit.

You must confess Christ publicly.[2]

Termites in the Wood

Just as little termites eat out the core of a post, weakening it and causing it finally to collapse, so, too, little sins in our lives have the same effect if they are not dealt with. Outwardly we may appear to other people to be good, strong Christians. But what are we really like on the inside? What is our true condition?

When God calls His people to *turn from their wicked ways,* we may think, "What? This cannot apply to me! There is nothing wicked in me!" We may think these words are too strong. But we fail to see that every small departure from God's way of holiness is sin. And sin, no matter how small and unimportant it may seem to be, is "wicked," because (like tiny termites) it spoils God's highest and best purpose for us. Little sins can eat out our spiritual strength and vitality without us realizing it. These sins must be identified so that we can repent of them and find forgiveness, release and revival. Are you prepared to pay the price for this? That's where revival begins!

For Further Reflection

1. Read Psalms 24:1–6; 51:1–17.
2. According to Psalm 24, what four things are required of those who would "ascend the hill of the LORD . . . and stand in his holy place" (Psalm 24:3)? What does each mean?
3. Real repentance must deal with specific sins. Prayerfully again go over the items listed in the study. Ask God to reveal anything in your life that may be grieving His

93

Spirit. Use the prayer of Psalm 139:23–24 to guide you. Tick anything God puts His finger on (no matter how small it may seem to be). Confess each one to God. Ask for His forgiveness and cleansing. Then ask for a change of heart and a willingness (with His help) to turn from these things and to live the way He wants you to live.

4. Psalm 51 is a psalm of repentance. Read verses 1–17 through again and make it your own prayer, expressing each verse in your own words. What parts of this psalm speak to you with the most meaning?

5. If you need to put things right with other people, deal with them as soon as possible. (See Matthew 5:23–24.) This might mean going to someone, saying sorry, apologizing, making a confession, writing a letter, making restitution or repayment or something else. What is God telling you to do?

6. Think about Evan Roberts's "four points," which were the basis of the Welsh revival. How do these apply personally to your own life?

13

CORPORATE REPENTANCE

A great shaking is occurring in the church. Dead traditions, prayerlessness, disunity and divisions are all crumbling like houses of clay in an earthquake. God is rumbling through Christianity.

Francis Frangipane, *The Days of His Presence*

Some sins are individual, but others are corporate. Sins that have affected the Body of Christ must be recognized, confessed and repented of before there can be revival. When we compare ourselves with one another or with other churches, we fail to see our true condition. We become used to the Christianity we have grown up with. We may have accepted things as they are and not realized the things that are draining our spiritual strength and making us weak and ineffective. Sins affecting the Body may remain hidden for years and never be dealt with. But a time of judgment is coming—God will suddenly come to His temple to cleanse and purify His people.

Where Judgment Must Begin

God must first deal with His Church before He can change society. Judgment must first begin with the family of God before God can heal our nation (see 1 Peter 4:17). The Church is the key to God's blessings coming upon our land. That is why God is calling His Church to wake up, to recognize her true condition and to repent!

The living Lord made clear what the churches of Asia Minor were to repent of (see Revelation 2–3). He revealed their true condition. Five of the seven churches had areas of failure and decline. They were each told to repent and return to the place where they should always have been. But if that was true then, what about now? What is the Spirit saying to His Church today? What kinds of things would He put His finger on? What would He say we need to repent of now?

What Should We Repent Of?

As a Church, repentance is needed in three main areas. These have to do with where we have fallen short in (1) our relationship with Christ (as Head), (2) our relationships within the Body (as members) and (3) our relationship with the world. In each of these areas we need to ask God to show us where we have fallen short of His plan for us, where we are grieving His Spirit and where we need to repent.

Where we have failed in our relationship with Christ

Have we lost our love and passion for Jesus—like the church at Ephesus? (See Revelation 2:4–5.) Yet this is the very heart of our relationship with God. Lose this, and no matter how hard we try, we have lost the most precious thing. Most Christians would admit that other things have crowded into their lives and they have lost the fervor and love for Jesus they once had. Have you? And when we lose our passion for Jesus, we lose our passion for worship. We can sing the songs, say the prayers, speak the words of adoration, listen to the Word of God, but our hearts are far away (see Matthew 15:8). Is that true of you? And how much has our worship on Sundays become an event with little influence on our lives during the rest of the week?

96

And what about prayer? What place does prayer have in the life of your church? And what place does it have in your own life? Are you praying and seeking God's face? Are you really depending on the presence and leading of the Holy Spirit? Or are you trusting in self-effort and programs to do God's work? Many churches are so organized and controlled that if the Holy Spirit withdrew, they would continue just the same. They have become so independent of the Holy Spirit that they don't even realize they have grieved—and even quenched—Him! As God's people we need to repent of our pride, independence and insensitivity to the Holy Spirit and give the Church back to Him. We need to repent of our prayerlessness and self-sufficiency and seek God's face afresh so that He can come and release His power among us (see 2 Chronicles 16:9).

Where we have failed in our relationships within the Body

Jesus has commanded us as His disciples to love one another (see John 13:34–35). He has also prayed that we might be one, as He and the Father are one (see John 17:20–21). Yet, for the most part, Christians are divided. There are over nine thousand Christian denominations throughout the world. Churches in the same region may have nothing to do with each other and may even work in opposition. This is one of the biggest obstacles to unbelievers coming to faith in Christ. Many churches are broken by divisions within. A divided Church will not have much appeal to a divided world. A sick Church cannot offer healing to a sick world. The Church can offer a reconciling and healing ministry to a divided and broken world only when she has first experienced it within her *own* ranks. How can God bless us when we do not love, accept and forgive one another? Disunity prevents the Holy Spirit from working. We must repent of the deep divisions spoiling our testimony and pray for the healing and renewing power of the Holy Spirit to unite us again as the Body of Christ.

Where we have failed in our relationship with the world

Jesus also prayed that we would go into the world but be kept from the evil one (see John 17:15–19). Yet how much have we let worldly attitudes and values influence us? Are we more concerned with seeking first material things than seeking first the Kingdom of God? Are we more concerned with building our church and our kingdom than building the Kingdom of God? What about the poor and needy around us? Do we really care? Are we making any real attempt to reach out to unbelievers with ministries of compassion and kindness? Or are we only really concerned about ourselves? Do we really have a burden for lost people like Jesus did? Then what are we doing about it? That was Jesus' mission. How committed are we to being a part of Jesus' commission to go out into the world to make disciples of all peoples? We need to repent in these areas where we have failed to do what Jesus has called us to do.

What Is God Saying to Us?

"He who has an ear, let him hear what the Spirit says to the churches" (Revelation 2:11). What is the Spirit saying to His Church today? What is He saying to your church? What is He saying to you? It is always easy at a human level to find fault with the Church and to be critical of her weaknesses and failings. But remember that the Church is made up of individuals like you and me. The safest way, then, is to begin by asking, "Lord, what are You saying to me? I am a part of the Body. So let Your Spirit convict me first of all and then convict us as a Body. Where do we need to repent and change?"

What do we need to repent of?

Look at the following list of items grouped under the three main areas outlined above. Tick any items where you believe you need to repent as a church (and as an individual).

Where we have failed in our relationship with Christ

☐ A lost love and devotion to Jesus (like the church at Ephesus)

☐ Little desire for prayer

☐ Prayerlessness—depending instead upon self-effort and programs

☐ Shallowness and often insincerity in our worship (with lips but not heart)

☐ Worship as an event (on Sundays) but not affecting life during the week

☐ Lack of faithfulness and obedience to the Word of God

☐ Lack of faithfulness in tithing and giving to God's work

☐ Little acknowledgment of and dependence on the Holy Spirit

☐ Little evidence of spiritual life and the Holy Spirit working

☐ Christian life and ministry dependent on self-effort

☐ The church controlled by people rather than by the Holy Spirit

☐ Church ruled by traditions more than by the Holy Spirit

☐ Complacency and lukewarmness (as in the church at Laodicea)

☐ Apathy—lost passion for Jesus and no concern for the lost

Where we have failed in our relationships within the Body

☐ Disunity and divisions among us (within and between churches)

☐ An independent spirit—indifference, suspicion, superiority, competitiveness

☐ Unconfessed grievances against each other

☐ Unwillingness to forgive each other

☐ Unconfessed and undealt-with wrongs in our past

☐ Lack of genuine love and care for one another

☐ Little concern to help the needy among us

☐ Legalism, Pharisaic or "religious spirit," criticism

☐ Authoritarian and controlling leadership

☐ People hurt by pastors and church leaders

☐ Pastors and leaders hurt by resistant and controlling church members

☐ Exalting our church (or denomination) while putting other churches down

☐ Little concern for other local churches and the wider Body of Christ

Where we have failed in our relationship with the world

☐ Worldly attitudes and values seeping into our lives

☐ More concerned with material interests than the Kingdom of God

☐ More concerned with buildings and facilities than with building people

☐ Little concern for the poor and needy

☐ Little attempt to reach out to unbelievers with caring ministries

☐ Little real concern for the lost

☐ Little concern for or commitment to world missions

Before there can be a worldwide harvest of souls into the Kingdom, God must first shake and wake up His Church. Before the glory of God can be revealed, God must first cleanse

His house. Before Christ comes again, His Bride must be made ready. And this is what God is doing! John Dawson says, "All over the world, tears of repentance are flowing. This is a day of God's merciful visitation."[1] Is that true of your church, of you?

God is bringing His Church to repentance. He is shaking out everything not centered in His Son. He is dealing with dead traditions, prayerlessness and disunity. This must happen before there can be revival. God in His mercy is cleansing and purging His Church. He is bringing her to brokenness and repentance and back to her first love, so that He can reveal His glory. Are you willing for God to do that in you too? Then ask that He give you (and your church) a deep spirit of repentance.

For Further Reflection

1. Read Malachi 3:1–5; Revelation 3:14–22. According to Malachi 3:1–5, how will God come to His people (His temple) and what will He do?

2. What is God saying to you? Go over the above lists again and ask, "Lord, what are You saying to me? I am a part of the Body. So let Your Spirit convict me first of all and then convict us as a Body." Deal with whatever the Lord puts His finger on—first of all at a personal level ("Lord, forgive me for —"). Then go on to confess on behalf of your church ("Lord, we have sinned against You in —").

3. If you are working through this study as a group, you may like to pause now and pray prayers of confession together based on the items you ticked above.

4. But repentance is not just confessing our wrongs; it is changing our behavior. As part of His Body, what is God calling you to do about the above areas?

5. Reread the quote by Francis Frangipane at the start of the chapter and then read the last two paragraphs at the

end of the chapter. What is God doing in His Church today? Why is He doing this? (See Hebrews 12:25–29.)

6. John Dawson says, "All over the world, tears of repentance are flowing. This is a day of God's merciful visitation." Is that happening in your church, and in you? How, then, can you come to this place of corporate repentance? What is God saying to you?

14

IDENTIFICATIONAL REPENTANCE

*We are called to live out the biblical practice of
identificational repentance, a neglected truth that
opens the floodgates of revival and brings healing
to the nations.*

John Dawson, *Healing America's Wounds*

John Dawson, in his book *Healing America's Wounds,* tells
of the time when he was asked to speak at a large women's
convention. He realized something deeper needed to be addressed than the topic he had planned to speak on:

It occurred to me that I could humble myself and ask forgiveness, as a male, for the multitudes of hurts inflicted on these
women by men. I was surrounded by stories of incest, rape,
rejection, betrayal and a multitude of other wrong actions by
men against women. Why not identify with these things, bring
them out into the open, confess that I knew only too well the
dark side of the masculine soul?[1]

This is what he did. He got up and with simple, faltering
words confessed the sins of men against women and asked for
forgiveness. He was amazed at the results. Floodgates of emotion
opened and the tears began to flow. After the meeting, women
approached Dawson with comments like "Something broke in

me when you said that." Another said, "You'll never know how much I needed to hear that." And the most common comment was, "Today is the first time I ever heard a man, any man, say, 'I'm sorry.'"[2]

This example brings us to the third level of repentance—*identificational repentance.* We have looked at individual and corporate repentance in the previous two chapters, but what is identificational repentance?

Identificational Repentance

The word *identification* means a willingness to join yourself to a group of people and to be counted as one of them. So the term *identificational repentance* means a willingness to identify yourself with the sins of a group of people (your family, church, gender, racial group, tribe or nation) and repent of those sins even though you may not have been personally responsible for them. You do this by owning and confessing their sins as yours and repenting on their behalf where they are unready or unable to do so themselves. (Isn't that exactly what Jesus did for us on the cross?)

We see examples of identificational repentance in Old Testament leaders like Nehemiah and Daniel. These men approached God in prayer by first acknowledging their own sin and the sins of their people. They included themselves as part of the sins of their forefathers and the sins of their nation, even though they may not have been personally guilty. They identified themselves with their people by saying, "*We* have sinned," rather than, "*They* have sinned."

Standing in the Gap

Ezekiel 22:30 says, "I looked for a man among them who would build up the wall and stand before me in the gap on behalf of the land so I would not have to destroy it, but I found none." The sins of the people had broken down the spiritual walls around their lives and left them wide open to the enemy's attacks (see verses 23–29). But God was looking for someone who would be willing to identify with the sins of the people and intercede for them, repent on their behalf and stand in the gap so that He could forgive, heal and restore. Otherwise, there could be no forgiveness, healing and reconciliation, and God's judgment would have to fall on them instead.

According to John Dawson, the walls of our spiritual lives are broken down, first, through *idolatry*.[3] Idolatry is a sin against God Himself. It is looking to other saviors instead of to Jesus, God's Son, to meet our needs. Idolatry breaks down our spiritual defenses and leaves us wide open to demonic spirits. Second, the spiritual walls are broken down through *injustice*. Satan finds entrance when people wound each other through selfish, sinful and unjust actions. Injustice opens the door for satanic oppression through unresolved anger, hostility, revenge and unforgiveness. People are powerless to deal with this outside of the cleansing, healing grace of God. But when a people cannot do this for themselves, who is going to stand in the gap on their behalf? Who is going to build up the wall again?

Only those who have first been reconciled to God themselves can stand in the gap on behalf of others. Unbelievers cannot go into the gap and present the blood of the Lamb. This is the privilege and responsibility of God's people alone. We are called to be priests (see 1 Peter 2:9). We are called to present the blood of Jesus before the Father for the sins of the people just as the ancient priesthood presented the blood of bullocks in making atonement for the nation. God is calling His people to this task of intercession, identificational repentance and reconciliation.

Owning the Sins of the Past

The greatest wounds in human history and the greatest injustices have not happened through the acts of some individual person alone. They have happened through groups of people inflicting wrongs on other groups of people. Because of this, we as individuals are tempted to clear ourselves of any personal responsibility. But God calls us as His people to stand in the gap. If we as believers (and priests) do not stand in the gap on behalf of our people to confess the wrongs committed, how will healing and reconciliation come? The wounds will remain unhealed and only go deeper. But when we repent on behalf of our people, church or group, this is the key that "opens the floodgates of revival and brings healing to the nations."

Wounding and injustice most commonly take place at the dividing lines of society: nation to nation, race to race, culture to culture, tribe to tribe, class to class, male to female, religion to religion, church to church, leaders to people, generation to generation, family to family and so on. Where these injustices and wrongs remain unconfessed and unhealed between such groups of people, the hurt continues, reconciliation never takes place and conflict deepens. Wounds that remain uncleansed and undealt with do not heal with the passing of time. They only remain under the surface and may break out again at any time. It is at these areas of wounding and injustice that we are called to stand in the gap through identificational repentance.

Repairing the Broken Walls

Not only are we to stand in the gap by seeking God's mercy and forgiveness on behalf of ourselves and our group, but we are also called to help repair the broken-down walls (see Isaiah

58:12). How do we do this? Four steps lead toward healing and restoring broken relationships:

- *Confession:* Acknowledging honestly the unjust or hurtful actions of myself or my people group toward other persons or groups of people.
- *Repentance:* Expressing deep sorrow, a repentant heart and turning from unloving to loving actions toward that person or group.
- *Reconciliation:* Seeking forgiveness and giving forgiveness and making attempts to develop closer fellowship with those who were against us.
- *Restitution:* Attempting to restore that which has been damaged or destroyed and seeking justice where injustice has prevailed.

Of the three levels of repentance we have looked at in the last few chapters—individual, corporate and identificational repentance—this third level of identificational repentance is probably the most difficult of all. Yet it is what Jesus did for us and what is desperately needed to bring healing at all levels of society. Are you willing to be a part of it?

For Further Reflection

1. Read Nehemiah 1:3–11; Daniel 9:4–19.
2. Jesus stood in the gap for us. What does He now call us to do? (See 2 Corinthians 5:18–20.)
3. Nehemiah and Daniel were willing to stand in the gap. What marks of identificational repentance are seen in their prayers? (See Nehemiah 1:3–11; Daniel 9:4–19.)
4. What kinds of things cause broken-down walls between us and God, and in our relationships with each other?

(Ezekiel 22:23–30 may give you some ideas.) What is God's solution? (See Ezekiel 22:30.)

5. Look back at the areas where wounding most commonly takes place. Is there some area where you know you could stand in the gap and start the process of healing and restoring broken relationships, through confession, repentance, reconciliation and restitution? What is God saying to you? What should you do?

PART 6

WHEN THE SPIRIT COMES IN POWER

God has promised in 2 Chronicles 7:14:

If my people, who are called by my name, will

- humble themselves (brokenness)
- pray (dependence)
- seek my face (intimacy)
- turn from their wicked ways (repentance)

Then will I

- *hear from heaven*
- forgive their sin
- heal their land

What happens when God *hears from heaven* and comes to heal our land? What should we expect? In the next three chapters we will look at this. You may be surprised to discover that when the Spirit comes in power, not everyone likes what happens!

15

WHAT SHOULD WE EXPECT?

Restrained! Quiet! Unobtrusive! My dear friends,
why not listen to the evidence? This is the kind of
thing that happens when the Spirit "comes" upon
man—even the building was shaken.

Martyn Lloyd-Jones, *Revival*

What should we expect when the Holy Spirit comes in revival? Many Christians pray for revival and long that God might come to awaken His Church. But when He comes in power it is not what they expected! What should we expect if God answers our prayers and sovereignly comes among us?

In the Solomon Islands in 1970, the Holy Spirit came upon a congregation in much the same way He did at Pentecost. During the time of quiet prayer following the message of a visiting evangelist, Muri Thompson, all heard the sound in the distance of what seemed like a wind but getting louder until it became a roar. One missionary looked out to see if the trees were moving—but the leaves were perfectly still. He thought, *Surely this is the Holy Spirit coming like a mighty rushing wind.* Then in a matter of seconds, the Holy Spirit fell upon all present and the silent church started to echo with wailing, praying and strong crying. As the leaders gave praise aloud, cries of conviction increased among the people. There was noise and commotion for quite some time and the meeting was out of human control. But gradually the people started to come through to deliverance. There was no panic; hardly any of those present moved from their seats. All was under the control of God. This was the start of a mighty move of God that spread to many parts of the Solomons.[1]

Revival Is Unpredictable

It is important to realize that the Spirit is sovereign and moves the way He chooses in each situation. He is unpredictable like the wind, and we cannot tell when He will come or how He will move (see John 3:8). This means not all revivals come in the same way. Not all revivals will start with the sound of a mighty wind as in the Solomon Islands revival. Every revival will be unique, though there will be common features to them all. It is dangerous, therefore, to read of one revival and to think all will be just like that. Even in the same revival movement there may be many different expressions and experiences. But one thing is sure—when revival comes, it is God breaking into our churches and into our lives in a powerful and perhaps unusual way. It is God revealing Himself to us in awesome holiness and great power. Revival is God coming to wake up careless and complacent Christians. It is God coming unexpectedly to His temple to cleanse and purify His people (see Malachi 3:1–4). Brian Edwards says, "We can never limit God in revival. The more we learn of His ways in revival, the less we can be sure of what He will do."[2]

Though the Holy Spirit may come in a variety of ways in revival, Martyn Lloyd-Jones describes what is central to the Holy Spirit coming in revival power. He says:

> It is an experience in the life of a church when the Holy Spirit does an unusual work. . . . Suddenly the power of the Spirit comes upon them and they are brought into a new and more profound awareness of the truths that they had previously

held intellectually, and perhaps at a deeper level too. They are humbled, they are convicted of sin, they are terrified at themselves. Many of them feel that they have never been Christians. And then they come to see the great salvation of God in all its glory and to feel its power. Then, as a result of their quickening and enlivening, they begin to pray. New power comes into the preaching of the ministers, and the result is that large numbers . . . are converted.[3]

Revival Brings Disturbance

Because revival comes suddenly, it will catch many by surprise. And it may not be what people expect. It will bring a shaking. It will cause disturbance. It will bring sudden changes. It will be God taking control. People will be profoundly affected. Leaders will have to release human control. There will be open and even noisy responses as God deals deeply with His people. There may be wailing and crying. People may shake or fall under deep conviction. We will see things we have never seen before. God's visitation will shake us out of our complacency. It will stir and challenge us deeply. It will deal strongly with the sins stopping God from blessing His Church and blessing us. It will overturn the normal order of things. Revival is not a soft and soothing presence of God that leaves us unchanged; it is God coming to wake and stir His Church, to refine and purify His people so that we might again be a holy people. Are you prepared for that?

Revival Brings an Extraordinary Harvest

True revival does not stay within the Church; it bursts out into the world. For part of God's purpose in pouring out His Spirit upon His people is to mobilize them for evangelism and mission (see Acts 1:8). Through revival He empowers and compels His people to get on with their primary task to "seek and to save the lost." The outpouring of the Spirit at Pentecost resulted in powerful witness and a mighty harvest with thousands of converts flooding into the Church. The same has happened again and again in revivals throughout history.

The plowman overtakes the reaper

Amos 9:13 gives a picture of what happens in times of revival: "'The days are coming,' declares the LORD, 'when the reaper will be overtaken by the plowman and the planter by the one treading grapes.'" In this picture given by Amos, the seed that was sown has resulted in such an abundant and supernatural harvest, that the plowman, who normally comes in to plow up the field again after the harvest is over, has to wait because the reaper is still trying to reap the enormous harvest! An ordinary sowing has resulted in an extraordinary reaping!

The Welsh revival (1904–1905)

Before the revival in Wales began, one church, for example, saw an increase of about 15 in its membership in one year. But in 1905 this same church had an increase of 318 members (more than twenty times as many!). Across Wales it is estimated that 20,000 people joined the churches during the first five weeks of the revival, and during the next two months, more than 80,000 responded to the Gospel. Within two years, as the revival spread to new areas, almost five million people were touched by it!

In revival the harvest reaches such overwhelming proportions that churches and Christian organizations are often unable to cope with the large numbers of people flooding in. One minister during revival said, "God has accomplished more in a single day of revival than I have accomplished during the whole of my ministry!"[4] We must still faithfully sow the seed, nurture and expect some kind of harvest under normal conditions. But in times of revival God sends an extraordinary and overwhelming harvest far beyond the normal.

Revival Brings Reaction

From a safe distance of several hundred years or several thousand miles, revival clearly looks exciting and wonderful. What could be more glorious than a mighty work of God in our midst, renewing Christians and converting thousands of unbelievers? The strange thing about revivals, however, is that while they are so longed for in times of barrenness, they are often opposed and feared when they arrive. Why? Because revival is threatening. It disturbs the established order of things. And this brings conflict, fear, division and even opposition from other Christians. Many things that happen in revival are unpredictable, untidy and emotionally messy. Revival changes our nice, orderly and controlled church services. People under the power of the Spirit do strange things and respond in strange ways. There may even be human extremes and excesses. Such happenings can upset people who want everything to be the way they like it—it can make them feel very uncomfortable. For these reasons many have opposed a genuine move of God when it comes.

Revival Means Spiritual Warfare

George Strachan, a former missionary in the Solomon Islands revival, says, "Most people speak of the blessing and benefits that come from revival. They are many indeed, but there are also battles. Revival is intense spiritual warfare."[5]

It is important to realize that every fresh activity and movement of the Spirit of God will be opposed by fallen human nature and the powers of darkness. Our natural self-life resists the Spirit (see Galatians 5:17). And Satan himself will challenge and oppose every advance of the Kingdom of God. He will do everything possible to hinder, spoil and destroy what God is doing. As revival progresses he will fight back. His plan is to divide Christians against each other. He may attack the leaders of revival internally through discouragement and despair. He will try to set leaders of the revival against each other in order to divide and conquer. He may overbalance the zeal of converts and cause them to run to fleshly extremes. And he will sow the counterfeit among the genuine things God is doing to cause confusion.

Because of all these things, when the Spirit comes in revival, not all will accept or welcome it. Revival leaders of the past, such as Jonathan Edwards, Charles Finney, John Wesley and Evan Roberts, all experienced great opposition and criticism especially from ministers and leaders within the Church. In the Solomon Islands revival, not all churches accepted it, and even some long-standing missionaries at first opposed it. This has been true through all the great revivals of history. So be prepared! Learn to recognize the genuine move of God and, when it comes, do not miss the day of divine visitation.

For Further Reflection

1. Read Malachi 3:1–5; Acts 4:23–31. According to these two passages, what are the results of the Lord coming in His manifest presence to His people?
2. Reread the story of the Solomon Islands revival at the start of this chapter. Should we expect all revivals to start like this? (See John 3:8.) What should we expect?
3. Look at the quotation by Martyn Lloyd-Jones at the start of the chapter and also on page 112. If the Spirit came in revival power upon your church congregation, what would you expect?
4. Amos 9:13 gives a picture of what happens in times of revival. What do you think this verse means? Look at

what happened in the Welsh revival of 1904–5. Imagine this happening in your church and other churches in your community. How well would your church cope with a flood of converts like this?

5. The strange thing about revivals is that while they are so longed for in times of barrenness, they are often commonly opposed and feared when they arrive. Why do you think this is?

6. Every fresh activity and movement of the Holy Spirit will be opposed by fallen human nature and the powers of darkness. Look at the following verses and write down the cause of this conflict: Luke 11:21–22; John 10:10; Galatians 5:17.

7. If revival means spiritual warfare, what else would you expect to take place with any genuine move of God?

16

THE FEAR OF REVIVAL

*Revival is a time when spiritual forces are un-
leashed—on both sides—and we must expect the
genuine and the counterfeit in spiritual phenomena.*

Brian Edwards, *Revival*

Revival is not always welcomed. Though we may long
for revival in times of spiritual barrenness and dryness,
we may be afraid of it or even oppose it when it arrives. Why
is this? There may be many reasons why people close their
hearts to revival when it comes.

Fear of Change

There is within each of us a resistance to change. The
older we grow, the less we cope with it. We like to stay the
way we are. We are comfortable with what we know and
believe. We do not like disturbance. Yet that is exactly what
revival does. It brings change. It stirs us from our comfort.
It challenges our halfhearted devotion. It uncovers our
sinfulness and selfishness. It calls us to rise and follow
Christ with a new zeal, devotion and obedience. But if we
are comfortable the way we are, we are not going to like
revival, for our self-life will resist whatever the Spirit is calling us to do (see Galatians 5:17). That is the very reason we

need revival—we need to change. Jesus is calling us back from living at a subnormal level to the "normal" Christian life. He is calling us back to intimacy with Himself so that we will have life and have it in all its fullness. This will be worth all the disturbance and difficulties we may experience in the process. To obtain this pearl of great price is worth everything we have.

Fear of Disorder

Another fear some may have about revival is that our orderly services will be overturned and disturbed by noise, emotion, crying and unpredictable events. After all, isn't the Scripture clear that everything is to be done "decently and in order" (1 Corinthians 14:40)? Commenting on the revival in New England in the early eighteenth century, Jonathan Edwards wrote, "Some object against it as great confusion . . . and say, God cannot be the author of it; because he is the God of order, not of confusion."[1]

Sometimes we confuse order with peace, quietness and a controlled program and think there is confusion when these are absent. Jonathan Edwards considered it no more confusion than if a group of people should meet in the field to pray for rain and then be disturbed from their praying by a heavy shower. The criticisms of John Wesley, George Whitefield and many past revival movements have sometimes been based on the wrong understanding of order. The stories of past revivals are full of descriptions of people weeping, shaking, crying out, falling down and sometimes becoming deeply troubled. Such events can threaten us and cause fear, because they are strange and unfamiliar. If we think that revival must be "decent and orderly" (and define this as meaning quietness, human control and predictability), then we do not understand what revival is and cut ourselves off from what has happened in nearly every revival in history.

Fear of Emotion

Many Christians have grown up in church traditions (and perhaps homes) that have told them to keep their emotions under tight control. Research has shown that while giving way to emotional feelings can sometimes be harmful and destructive, many are sick because of repressed and over-controlled emotions. Sometimes we need to rejoice without holding back, or to weep freely, if that is needed, to release inner tensions and come to emotional health.

We should not be afraid of emotion but *emotionalism*. Emotions are the natural feelings that arise within us in response to what is happening around or within us. But emotionalism is the stirring up of emotions in order to make people respond in certain ways. When others try to stir or control our emotions, this can lead to all kinds of extremes and excesses. But when the Holy Spirit awakens people in times of revival, He seems to release people in the area of their emotions. In God's presence people tremble, cry out, shout, weep, rejoice, stand or fall with fear and awe. God is doing something deeper than just touching the mind; He is dealing with the whole person. In fact, Jonathan Edwards was convinced that nothing of spiritual importance ever took place in a human heart if it was not deeply touched by such godly emotions. He claimed that feelings express the soul's response to God. Without them a deep change of life was not likely to follow. In revival, the hard heart is made tender again (the releasing of people's emotions is often a sign of this), and a tender heart is open to spiritual truth and the Spirit's working.

Fear of Excesses

Sometimes strange things happen in revival and people go to extremes. People can focus on the strange parts of revival and be caught up with them more than they are caught up with Jesus. Critics of revival will often point to the extremes of what is happening and use such examples to reject it all as false. Such reports can quickly fan fear in others and cause rejection of even a genuine work of God.

It is important to realize that revival is never pure. The river of God will always stir up mud along its banks. There will always be those who go to fleshly extremes and bring dishonor on the whole. And there will always be critics who make much of this. Judge a move of God by its center, not by its extremes! What is the fruit? Is there faithfulness to the Word of God? Is there deep sorrow over sin and a turning away from it? Are people's lives being changed? Are they more in love with Jesus than before? Are they hungrier for His Word? Have their hearts been set on fire with a new love for Jesus? Is there a deepening desire for holiness? Do they have a new desire to serve God and win others for Christ? This is the center of any true move of God. If we focus on the failures of people touched by revival, we may miss the real thing. In looking at human weakness, we may fail to see what God is doing.

Fear of Error

Another fear is that people caught up in revival can let go of the Word of God and let feelings and experiences rule their lives. Without the foundation of Scripture to guide them, they can easily move off balance into extremes and even into error. This has happened in revivals in the past and can happen again. Because of this fear, some would pull back and resist revival or anything that challenges their theology or touches people emotionally.

This is a real and understandable fear. The Word of God must always be the foundation of our lives. Emotions and spiritual experiences must always be tested and kept in line with the teachings of Scripture. Many Christians have moved

WHEN THE SPIRIT COMES IN POWER

into error because they have not held to biblical truth nor understood its breadth and balance. This is why biblical teaching and discipleship training are so important before and during times of revival. John Wesley during the revival in England made sure those awakened by revival were joined into small discipleship groups (see chapter 23). George Strachan, a missionary during the Solomon Islands revival of 1970, believes that one of the main factors that prepared the South Seas Evangelical Church for revival and has kept the revival fires burning for so long after 1970 was the in-depth teaching of the Word of God.

Revival brings the fire, but the Word of God provides the fuel to keep the fire burning. Revival creates spiritual hunger, but the Word of God provides the food to satisfy that hunger. Without the Word of God, revival can quickly die or leave people with spiritual anemia and malnutrition. Rather than resisting revival and preventing Christians from coming alive and hungering for more of God, the better solution is to go with revival and make sure their hunger is satisfied and their lives nourished with a balanced diet from the Word of God. Only this will keep them from error and enable them to grow from spiritual babyhood to maturity.

Fear of Losing Control

This fear especially operates at the level of church leadership. Throughout history pastors have either been great friends or great enemies of revival. For a pastor, a genuine revival can either be a source of wonderful joy or a cause of great upset and anxiety. While some pastors would gladly welcome a move of the Holy Spirit in revival, others would strongly oppose it. Any pastor should rightly oppose extremes and errors in revival movements. But opposition is often to the genuine work of God itself. Why should this be? Perhaps it is because revival challenges their spiritual shallowness and narrow theology.

They just cannot accept that God may work differently to what they believe or have experienced. Revival also threatens those who want to maintain their own positions of importance or influence within the Church. So they fight against anything that challenges their authority and control. For these reasons the religious leaders crucified Jesus and persecuted the early disciples. And this is why revivals have always caused argument and opposition, right up to today.

For Further Reflection

1. Read Luke 11:14–20; Acts 4:1–22. How did the religious leaders respond to Jesus and His disciples? Why do you think they responded like this?
2. What are some of the positive things you have heard or experienced about revival, and what are some of the negative things? List these.
3. According to the quote by Brian Edwards at the start of the study, why do you think we see both good and bad elements in revival?
4. What should our attitude be toward any so-called move of God when we hear of excesses or extremes? Should we reject it all as false (or even of the devil)? What should we do?
5. List the key things you would expect to see at the heart of a revival if you are to be convinced this is a true work of God.
6. At a personal level, are you afraid of some of the changes revival may bring to your life? What changes are you most afraid of and why? How can you deal with these fears so as not to miss revival when it comes?

17

THE PHENOMENA OF REVIVAL

*Physical responses have probably been the most
debated part of the history of revivals.*

Brian Edwards, *Revival*

During the revivals in the time of John Wesley and George Whitefield, we read of unusual things happening. John Wesley recorded this in his journal (July 7, 1739):

> No sooner had Whitefield begun to invite all sinners to believe in Christ than four persons sunk down close to him almost in the same moment. One of them lay without sense or motion. A second trembled exceedingly. The third had strong convulsions all over his body but made no noise unless by groans. The fourth, equally convulsed, called upon God with strong cries and tears. From this time I trust we shall allow God to carry on His own work in the way that pleases Him.[1]

As we look at revivals past and present, we see that with them come strange behaviors. The accounts of revivals are full of stories of people weeping, shaking violently, crying out, losing consciousness, falling down, laughing or acting in other strange ways. These things have brought two opposite reactions from people. Some totally reject all that takes place and so miss out on the fresh blessings and deeper things God is doing. On the other hand, others blindly accept everything without discernment and are in danger of being deceived by

Satan or misled by the flesh. How are we to understand these strange responses or phenomena? Are they a part of the genuine work of God in revival, or are they not?

Three Possible Explanations

In any revival, as well as the true work of the Holy Spirit, we see human or fleshly responses and also the false work of Satan, who tries to distort and deceive. But how can we know the difference?

The genuine work of God

Falling down, trembling and crying out or appearing like dead men seem to have been natural reactions of people in Scripture who met with God in a close way (see Isaiah 6:1–8). When the Holy Spirit filled the first disciples on the Day of Pentecost, some people in the crowd thought they were drunk (see Acts 2:13). Their actions were not what you would normally expect of people in control of themselves. In times of revival, when people are touched powerfully and filled with the Spirit of God, unusual responses may be seen. In fact, in almost every revival in history, stories of strange physical manifestations are recorded. If revival is God coming in unusual power to wake, shake, purge and renew His people, we should expect some unusual things to happen. And they do! When God moves powerfully in revival, He touches the whole person. So we should expect that this will show itself in emotional and physical ways as well.

Richard Crisco, youth pastor in the Pensacola, Florida, revival in the Brownsville Assemblies of God, makes these comments:

> When people go down under the power of God, we have observed how the Holy Spirit has taken control, and He is speaking to them. He is speaking purpose. He is speaking hope.

125

Many times He is just bathing them in His love and putting a yearning for Him inside their hearts. . . . I have seen young ladies lying on the floor . . . shaking and wailing. In those moments, God has healed them of painful memories of rape or other types of abuse. Many times as people are being shaken by the power of God on the outside, He is shaking things loose on the inside. He is tearing things out of them—sins they have committed, and sins that have been committed against them. He is just ripping them loose and setting them free.[2]

"Fleshly" imitations

Where God is moving powerfully and doing a genuine work in people's lives, we can also expect fleshly imitations and satanic counterfeits to soon appear. Our impure human responses and Satan's direct interference will soon muddy the pure waters. This is where spiritual discernment is needed.

In meetings conducted by John and Charles Wesley, powerful manifestations of the Spirit were seen. But they also noticed fleshly imitations. John Wesley records the following comment in his journal:

Many, no doubt, were, at our first preaching, struck down both body and soul, into the depth of distress. Their outward responses were easy to be imitated. . . . Today, one was pleased to fall into a fit for my entertainment, and beat himself heartily. I thought it a pity to hinder him; so left him to recover at his leisure. Another girl, as she began to cry, I ordered to be carried out. Her convulsion was so violent, as to take away the use of her limbs, till they laid and left her outside the door. Then immediately she found her legs and walked off.[3]

It is a natural human response to want to be included when God is touching other people in unusual ways. Some might think, *Why isn't this happening to me? Why isn't God touching me in the same way?* This fear of missing out can make some people try to copy (either consciously or unconsciously) what

126

God is doing in others. But this will only leave you unsatisfied and empty.

Satanic counterfeits

Remember that revival means intense spiritual warfare. Brian Edwards says, "Revival is a time when spiritual forces are unleashed—on both sides—and we must expect the genuine and the counterfeit in spiritual phenomena." Satan will always oppose what God is doing. When the Spirit is present in power, Satan will be all the more active to deceive and confuse, trying to spoil what God is doing. Some think this proves that the work is itself satanic rather than from God. But Satan's activity may prove the very opposite. The presence of the counterfeit means there is also the real thing to be copied. John Wesley was not surprised when demons manifested themselves in some of his revival gatherings. Where Satan's control over people's lives is strong, and where witchcraft and spirit worship are practiced, satanic manifestations are sure to appear. Both Scripture and history teach us that (see Luke 4:31–37).

God Deals Personally

It is a wonderful thing to realize that when the Holy Spirit moves corporately, He still deals with us individually. God is a God of variety and this is true even in revival. He does not work in the same way with us all. (In fact, if the responses are all the same, it is probably more of man than of God!) In a genuine move of God some will feel divine power flowing through them. Others may not. Some will show outward responses. Others will be unaffected. Each will respond in a variety of ways. But not all will experience the same thing. And this may have nothing to do with lack of openness to God (although a closed, hard or skeptical heart will certainly miss what God is doing). Some who love the Lord deeply and long for revival may not seem to be touched at all! But God knows our hearts and deals with us according to our need. So don't try to imitate the way He is working in another. Just let Him work in you the way He pleases, and let your response be only what He is genuinely doing.

The Real Test of Phenomena

The real test of a true move of God is not the presence of strange behaviors but the fruit of changed lives. Are people more in love with Jesus than they were before? Are they hungrier for His Word? Is there a turning away from sin? Do they long to be in God's presence? Do they have a new desire for prayer? Are they growing in holiness of life? Do they have a new burden to bring others to Christ? The important thing is not that you shake or quake! It is not that you shiver or quiver! It is not that you fall or crawl! The important thing is: Is your life changed? The phenomena are outward, short-lived, passing and in themselves of no lasting importance. That is why they tend to disappear as revivals go on. The real test of revival is fruit—and fruit that lasts (see John 15:16). There may be immediate changes, but the real test is six or twelve months later. How different are you then? Is there continuing growth and change in your life? Is Jesus now the central desire of your heart? Nothing else counts in the end, and that is the final test of any true move of God.

For Further Reflection

1. Read Isaiah 6:1–5; Daniel 10:4–12. What effect did God's powerful presence have on these people?
2. Reread the journal entry of John Wesley at the start of the chapter. In thinking about these strange responses in revival, what two opposite reactions must we be care-

ful to avoid? Why must we be careful not to go to these opposite extremes?

3. Look at some more biblical examples of people who were confronted with the glory of God. What effect did this have on them? Ezekiel (Ezekiel 1:28), the disciples (Acts 2:13), Saul (Acts 9:3–9), John (Revelation 1:12–17).

4. Think about fleshly imitations. Why do you think some people would want to imitate (whether consciously or unconsciously) the signs of what God is doing in the lives of others?

5. When God comes in a divine visitation upon His people, would you expect Him to work in the same way with each person? What would you expect to happen?

6. Why was John Wesley not surprised to see demonic activity in his meetings, and why should we not be startled either? (See Luke 4:34, 41.)

7. What is the real test that God is touching people's lives (and yours) in a deep way? Are the physical responses important, or is it something else? (See John 15:16.)

PART 7

THE FRUIT
OF REVIVAL

In Part 6 we looked at what happens when the Spirit moves
in power. Revival is often accompanied by unusual phenomena—some, a natural response to the Spirit's powerful
presence, and others, perhaps self-induced or even Satan's
counterfeit. How can we know what is truly of God?

The focus should never be on the manifestations of revival.
These will come and go. The real test of revival is the fruit of
changed lives—and fruit that lasts. It is not the shaking or
quaking that is important but a deep change of heart and life.
What, then, is the fruit of revival? In the next three chapters
we will look at the results of a genuine move of God.

18

A REVIVAL OF PRAYER

*We must commit to loving Jesus more than any-
thing else in the world and be willing to reject
whatever keeps us at arm's length from the glory of
his presence.*

Wayne Jacobsen, *A Passion for God's Presence*

When the Moravian revival began among the Moravian community at Herrnhut in Germany in 1727, Christians had a new desire to pray as never before. They committed themselves to pray around the clock, covering the 24 hours of each day in prayer. Within a month even children were holding their own prayer meetings, spending many hours in "praying, singing and weeping." This continuous chain of prayer continued for a hundred years—the longest recorded prayer meeting in history!

One result of the revival in Ulster in 1859 was the rapid growth of prayer meetings. In one district alone, a hundred weekly prayer meetings commenced. During this revival, prayer meetings could be found everywhere—even in grave-yards and gravel pits! One large Presbyterian church was crowded to overflowing with people wanting to pray, and this was on Saturday, the weekly market day, when normally fewer than a dozen would come to pray!

One of the great marks of the 1904 revival in Wales was the meetings for prayer that resulted, and not just in churches but deep underground where many worked in the coal mines. Stories were reported of workmen on night shift going to work half an hour early in order to pray together. One report describes eighty workmen meeting for prayer in a horse stable at the bottom of a shaft with only a dim lamp to give them light. There these men, whose faces showed the scars of hard underground toil, "quivered with a new emotion" as they listened to the Scriptures, prayed and worshiped together before starting their night's work.[1]

New Longing for Prayer

Someone has called prayer *the great fruit of revival.* It is the first and most obvious change that revival brings. There are two parts to revival praying: praying for revival, and praying as a result of revival. Before revival, it may be only a few praying. From a human point of view, as we have seen, it seems that these prayers of a faithful few bring revival down. But the second part of revival praying is what happens to prayer when revival comes.

When revival comes, prayer becomes the deepest desire of the heart, and Christians just can't wait for times of prayer. Prayer meetings that before were poorly attended are now filled with praying Christians. There is now a new desire and longing to be in God's presence. People pray in churches, in places of work, in homes, on prayer mountains and other places specially set aside for prayer. Prayer is no longer a burden, though it may still be a battle. Rather, it becomes a delight. The records of revival are full of stories telling of the fresh life and enthusiasm Christians have for prayer in times of revival.

New Sense of God's Presence

It is important to realize that prayer during revival is not just an increase in the kind of praying experienced before revival. No, it is a new kind of prayer altogether. It has a new quality. It is filled with an awesome sense of God's presence. And it comes with a new awareness of God that brings a holy fear and deep reverence and awe.

Revival prayer is praying with heart hunger. It is praying with passion. It is praying with fire. And it is praying out of the prompting and movement of the Holy Spirit. No longer is it man-compelled or man-controlled praying. No longer is it "shopping-list" type of praying. It is Spirit-led praying that comes out of worship, waiting on God and listening to what the Spirit is saying. It no longer follows a fixed program; nor is it controlled by time. Rather, it is entering into the presence of God and praying out of the burden the Holy Spirit lays upon the hearts of His people and staying with it until it is done, even if that means waiting and watching all night!

Simultaneous Praying

Often in revival the burden of prayer wells up and over-whelms a congregation so that everyone prays out loud at the same time. This has been seen in revivals in Korea, Borneo, India, Wales, the South Pacific Islands and elsewhere.

In the Korean revival in 1907, the missionaries sensed this burden to pray welling up within the congregation, so the leader simply said, "If it helps you all to pray together, then pray in that way." A reporter describes what happened:

> Then a tide began to sweep through the church. There was no confusion; it was a single harmony of prayer, as if the voices of the entire praying congregation merged together to form a single cry to God. There was not the slightest disorder. The Holy Spirit welded them all together into one . . . all souls were tuned to the same note, and unity of the Spirit held sway.[2]

I have been in prayer meetings of this nature in the Solomon Islands. What an awesome experience to be part of a body of people pouring out their hearts together like this before God! The praying is like the roar of a mighty waterfall—so loud that you cannot even hear your own voice! It is powerful and deeply moving, a sign of the great burden for prayer that revival brings with it.

Some Christians may think this kind of praying strange, noisy or even out of order. But perhaps this is because we have lost something of the spontaneous heart for prayer the early Christians had after Pentecost. The early Christians "raised their voices together in prayer to God" (Acts 4:24). This sounds like simultaneous praying! And the underlying Greek word would support that idea. This kind of praying brings full participation and is powerful. It is not just one praying and everyone listening—it is all praying with only God listening. After all, isn't that what prayer is meant to be? Where hundreds have gathered with a strong desire to pour out their hearts before God, how could there be time for each to pray separately? And is there any need to wait? Who are we praying to? To others, or to God? His ear finds no difficulty in hearing the individual prayers of thousands (and even millions) praying at the same time.

Prayer in the Solomon Islands

Since the beginning of the Solomon Islands revival in 1970, it has been common practice in the village churches to have prayer times from 4:00 A.M. to 6:00 A.M. every morning before the people go to their day's work. There are also designated prayer mountains where groups and church fellowships go to pray. On one prayer mountain just outside the capital, Honiara, groups pray day and night. In fact, as one group worships and prays, the sound of other groups nearby on the mountain can be heard rising in the stillness of the night as they, too, worship and cry out to God together. What a moving experience to see a people who have such a passion to pray and such a desire to be in God's presence!

And what about their approach to prayer? They come with a sense of reverence and awe. There is no casual sauntering into the place of prayer, talking and chatting about other things—there is a hush and a sense of expectancy. And before entering the designated prayer area, time is often taken to respond to the leader's call for all present to prepare their hearts and to ensure nothing hinders their praying. They will worship and wait for perhaps half an hour, or even an hour, until they are all ready and united in heart before they begin praying. What a contrast to our casual approach to prayer in the West!

I have been on a prayer mountain with groups praying till the early hours of the morning and even right through till dawn. And what an experience! This is no shopping-list type of praying. It is worship, waiting, preparing one's heart, listening for the Spirit's voice and responding to the burdens and directions He may give. It is battling at times against spiritual forces. It is at times noisy. It is interlaced with songs and carried along by worship. It is unpredictable, for there is no agenda. It may go on till 1:00 or 2:00 A.M., or, if the Spirit is moving, continue through the night! There have been times when young people have spent the whole of Saturday night on a prayer mountain and come straight from a night of prayer into the morning service hot with the presence of God! And what a powerful impact that has had on the morning service! What I have witnessed and experienced on these prayer mountains has changed my life and my whole understanding of what corporate prayer could and should be.

Are the Results of Revival Transferable?

In reading of these experiences and stories of revival, there is always the temptation to think we must copy these results if we

137

want to see revival here. We can make the mistake of seeking the results of revival rather than seeking the source of revival—Jesus Himself. We can learn from churches in revival how to seek God more earnestly, but no amount of copying the outcome of revival will bring revival itself. It is not new methods we need but a fresh encounter with Jesus. When God brings revival to our land, He will do it His own way and the fruit will be uniquely ours, not a photocopy of the way He has worked elsewhere.

For Further Reflection

1. Read Acts 4:23–31. What special marks do you notice in this early Church prayer meeting? How did they pray and what was the outcome?
2. One of the first and most obvious changes revival brings is in the area of prayer. What main changes does revival bring?
3. Look at the three examples at the start of the chapter. Do you think this longing and commitment to prayer would have taken place if there had not first been a visitation of the Spirit upon these people? What are the signs that God had done something deep in the lives of these people?
4. Think about the way people often break into simultaneous and united praying in times of revival. (See Acts 4:24.) Why do you think this happens? Why is this kind of praying so powerful?
5. Prayer in the Solomon Islands: Reread this section. Underline any words or phrases that show these people have been touched by true revival. How do you feel as you read this account?
6. Remember, you do not have to wait till revival comes to seek God in prayer. God calls you to come now. What has God been saying to you through this study, and how should you respond?

19

A REVIVAL OF WORSHIP

Revival will always do something to our worship. When our hearts are set on fire, our worship is going to be different.

Ian Malins

J oseph Kemp, who visited Wales in 1905, reported on what deeply impressed him there. He said:

In Wales I saw the people had learned to sing in a way which to me was new. I never heard such singing as theirs. They sang such old familiar hymns as "When I survey the wondrous cross," and "There is a fountain filled with Blood," and "I need Thee, oh, I need Thee." They needed no organist or choir or leader. Their singing was natural. The Holy Spirit was in their singing as much as in any other exercise. They had the New Song. People tell us our religion is joyless. Well, if the saints of the Living God have no joy, who has? Jesus Christ has given us to see that joy is one of the qualities He imparts to the saints of God. The world knows nothing of it. . . . When a revival from God visits a congregation it brings with it joy.[1]

In the last chapter we saw the first fruit of revival is a revival of *prayer*. And closely joined to this is a revival of *worship*. Revival will always do something to our worship. When our hearts are set on fire, our worship is going to be different in several ways.

Joy and Singing

Singing has always been part of the worship of God. It is to be expected, then, that when revival comes, songs of joy will fill our hearts and mouths. Old hymns and songs will have new meaning and depth, and we will sing them from the heart. God will give new songs to express the new thing He is doing and the deep love and longing in our hearts. Our singing will come alive. The deep repentance and sorrow over sin that first come with revival will soon give way to rejoicing "with an inexpressible and glorious joy" (1 Peter 1:8).

An Awesome Sense of God's Presence

With revival comes an awesome sense of God's presence. If there is one part of worship that is lacking in many churches today, it is the felt presence of God. We just go on with our worship, believing God is with us, yet rarely sensing His presence in a powerful way. But in revival it is altogether different—God is not only believed to be there; He is *known* to be there. His presence becomes so real that at times it is overwhelming. Even unbelievers are compelled to admit, "God is really among you."

Welsh revival

Rhys Bevan Jones describes one of the most powerful meetings he ever experienced in Wales in 1904:

> The whole place at that moment was so awful with the glory of God—one uses the word "awful" deliberately; the holy presence of God was so manifested that the speaker himself was overwhelmed; the pulpit where he stood was so filled with the light of God that he had to withdraw! There, let us leave it at that. Words cannot describe such an experience.[2]

140

God's presence may not always be as powerful as in this example, but in times of revival His presence among His people is known and felt. This will bring various responses. At times it will mean joyful celebration that may be loud and noisy with clapping, raising of hands, dancing and other physical expressions. But the sense of God's closeness will also bring deep reverence and awe as people respond to Him from their hearts. Tears will often flow in worship as people experience God touching their lives. When people are truly caught up in God's presence, they forget about themselves and others and become lost in wonder, love and praise. Revival brings a new depth to worship and a new love and longing for Jesus. No longer is there a casual or careless approach to worship. There may be joy, but there is no joviality. A holy seriousness is a constant feature of the way people approach God in true revival.

Solomon Islands revival

One strong feature of the revival in the Solomon Islands that struck me was the reverence and awe in the place of worship. Some churches had the practice of first gathering the people together outside the church entrance to offer prayers of cleansing and preparation before entering silently into the church building. And sometimes they would even remove their shoes before doing so. The strong message in this was, "This is holy ground; the presence of God is here."

Then, inside the church, there was a quietness as people prepared for worship. No chatter—they could do that later. They were there to meet with God. I have even seen rows of small children sitting on their own down the front, who before were running noisily outside playing games, now sitting unsupervised in silence and then joining in the songs of praise and worship, singing with all their hearts. Little wonder that the presence of God comes in such gatherings! These people have tasted revival and take the presence of God seriously. I have felt the presence of God moving in those humble gatherings in ways I have never experienced in my own country, Australia.

141

A Longing to Worship

The third aspect of revived worship is the longing in believers' hearts to meet with God. People can't wait to come to the place of worship in order to experience the wonderful presence of God. In revival, people long to be near God, and they want to stay there. Whereas before revival came, time was important; now time seems not to matter. In more than one revival the claim was made that "clocks have gone out of fashion." Before revival the difficulty was to get people into church, but now it is hard to get them out!

Iain Murray describes the typical response of people to revival during the ministry of Martyn Lloyd-Jones in Wales in 1931:

> On a Sunday evening the building would start to fill as much as an hour before the 6.30 hour of service, with sometimes not a seat remaining empty by 6 p.m. The Monday and Wednesday meetings had to be in the church itself on account of the numbers attending. Shopkeepers would arrive straight from their business without an evening meal. Night-shift workers, due to report for work at 8.30 p.m., would come in their working clothes, preferring to miss part of the meeting rather than the whole.[3]

In revival, the length of services no longer matters. If the Spirit of God is moving in the meeting, people will stay as long as needed for Him to do whatever He wants to. There is a sense of expectancy and excitement. Now the event and not the time is most important. If people are experiencing the felt presence of God and being touched by Him, time does not matter. If that is not happening, time is important. Time alone will not bring the Holy Spirit's presence and activity. A long service without the Holy Spirit's presence is wearisome. Worship and preaching without the Spirit is lifeless and dead. But when the Holy Spirit is moving, that all changes, and people do not want to leave. Brian Edwards sums it up in this way:

Today we have a carelessness in our churches, where many will not attend more than one service in a day. . . . In revival the churches are overcrowded with people who only attend once—not because the congregation will not turn out for the evening, but because they will not go home in the morning![4]

For Further Reflection

1. Read Psalms 95; 96:1–9. When we experience God's presence among us, how should this affect us? (See Psalms 95:6–7; 96:8–9.)
2. Look at Joseph Kemp's report of the Welsh revival at the start of the chapter. What changes did revival bring to their worship?
3. An awesome sense of God's presence: Reflect again on the second section in the chapter. What most noticeable changes does revival bring to worship? How does this compare with what you experience in worship?
4. Reread the account of the Solomon Islands revival in the second section of the chapter and underline the words or phrases that describe how these Solomon Island people approach worship. How does this speak to you? What is God saying to you about your attitude toward worship? (See Psalm 46:10 and Matthew 15:8–9.)
5. A longing to worship: Have you ever attended church services where there has been as much eagerness for worship as we see in the example of Martyn Lloyd-Jones in the chapter? Why do you think people are so eager to come to church meetings in times of revival?
6. What has God been saying to you through this chapter? Take a few moments to express back to God in prayer whatever longing or desire you have within your heart.

20

HOLINESS AND HARVEST

God is a God of mission. He sends revival not only to awaken us to Himself, but to awaken us to the needs of a lost and dying world.

Ian Malins, *Understanding Our Need of Revival*

On June 18, 1995, the fire of God fell on the Brownsville Assemblies of God Church in Pensacola, Florida. The strong feature of this revival was repentance and holiness of life, with people literally running to the altar to get right with God. All this happened at a time when the senior pastor was struggling with his ministry. He felt spiritually dry and was burdened with the daily demands of running the church. For eighteen months there had been daily persistent praying, and the pastor, John Kilpatrick, had set aside hours each day for prayer and intimacy with God. Then, on this day in 1995, God took over his life and his church. And over the four years following, well over two million people visited Pensacola to witness the revival for themselves, and more than 120,000 people responded to altar calls. This included first-time conversions as well as many rededicating themselves to Christ after backsliding or just drifting aimlessly in their Christian lives.

In the previous two chapters we began looking at the lasting fruit of revival. We saw that true revival is more than just exciting times with unusual things happening. True revival brings a revival in prayer, and it brings a revival of worship.

But there are two more results of a genuine move of God. True revival must always bring a revival of holiness, and it results in mission and harvest.

A Revival of Holiness

An elder in the Borneo church commented on the change he had witnessed soon after revival began in 1973. He said:

> The services are so different from what I have ever experienced before. When the Holy Spirit comes down upon the congregation, people begin to cry out in loud wailing (sometimes twenty or thirty people at the same time) calling out to God for forgiveness of sins and some calling the names of people with whom they have been quarrelling in a desperate desire to get reconciled. Many pending court cases have been cancelled because the parties involved have been reconciled in a very dramatic manner with tears and embraces of godly love. After the sin problems have been dealt with by the Lord and forgiveness granted, then the service goes on with loud singing of praises while tears of joy are still flowing down.[1]

True revival will always result in an awakening to the presence of sin, to deep conviction, to repentance, and result in a return to godly holiness. Revival can never be separated from holiness. If what people call revival is not leading them to deal with sin and return to holiness in obedience to God's Word, then we are not looking at revival. Revival always throws light into the dark and hidden areas of our lives. It reveals sin. It deals uncomfortably with those things the world accepts and that we do not see. It confronts us with our sin for what it really is and makes us want to turn away from it.

The Lord disciplines those He loves (see Hebrews 12:6). This discipline can come through the conviction of the Spirit, through correction from the Word of God and through times of hardship and suffering. The purpose of this discipline is that "we may share

145

in his holiness" (verse 10). Through revival God is waking and shaking His Church. He is shaking out all that is not centered on His Son—worldliness, idolatry, secret sins, human control, disunity. Remember, the Holy Spirit is *the Spirit of holiness.* His main purpose is to prepare us as Christ's Bride so that we become holy, radiant, without spot or blemish and blameless when Jesus comes again. His main work is to lead us into holiness so that we can enjoy sweet fellowship with Jesus now and be prepared for the heavenly Kingdom yet to come (see Hebrews 12:14).

Revival hastens this process of making us holy ("sanctification"). Without revival, our growth in holiness may take years— or never really happen at all. Without it we may remain weak, stunted Christians all of our lives. In revival the Spirit comes to wake us up and to reveal things as they really are. He can reveal in an instant wrong attitudes, actions and motives we had not seen before—things we did not even realize were hindering our growth. This does not mean that revival brings instant holiness or perfection; it simply wakes us up and gets us going and growing again toward God's perfect purpose for our lives.

A Revival of Mission

True revival does not stay within the Church; it bursts out into the world. Part of God's purpose in pouring out His Spirit upon His people is to move us into evangelism and mission (see Acts 1:8). In fact, if revival is kept within the Church, it will die. God is a God of mission. He sends revival not only to awaken us to Himself but to awaken us to the needs of a lost and dying world. Keep revival to yourself and you will lose it; give it away and you will continue to enjoy it.

The Moravian revival

When revival began among the Moravian community at Herrnhut, there was not only a burden to pray that continued unbroken for a hundred years but also a burden for mission. As a result, within the next sixty years these Moravians sent out over three hundred missionaries to almost every country in Europe and covered vast areas of North and South America, Asia and Africa. Half a century before William Carey went to India, the Moravians had spread the Gospel in places barely known. Someone has claimed that the Moravians achieved more in twenty years than the entire evangelical Church had done in two centuries! It is estimated, for example, that they won thirteen thousand converts in the West Indies before any other missionaries arrived. William Carey and John Newton were influenced by the lives of Moravian missionaries, and John Wesley was converted through the witness of Moravians.

Charles Finney in America

When Charles Finney was a young boy, there were only about two hundred thousand church members in the whole of the United States. But during the 1857 revival, there were up to fifty thousand conversions a week! When Finney visited Rochester, New York, a hundred thousand were added to the churches. Someone said to Finney at the time, "This is the greatest revival of religion that has been since the world began."[2] By 1859 there were at least five hundred thousand conversions, and a few years later when his work was finished, the number had risen to more than three million.

There are other amazing stories from past revivals. But throughout the twentieth century, and especially the past few decades, we have seen even more amazing things happening. In our time great numbers are being won into the Kingdom on a wider scale and across more countries of the world than we have ever seen before. And some of the greatest revivals are in places like South America, Africa and parts of Asia.

147

A New Thrust into Mission

True revival empowers us to fulfill the Great Commission (see Matthew 28:18–20). Outside of revival, Christians are reluctant to witness. But in times of revival, Christians go out eagerly—nobody can stop them! True revival is like a grass fire that catches and spreads wherever believers go. And this is what we should long for and expect when revival comes.

A revival of prayer, worship, holiness and mission are the central marks of what God does when His Spirit comes in revival. This is the fruit of true revival. If these things are not present or do not last, then it is not true revival, or something has gone wrong. How, then, do we maintain revival when it comes? This is what we will look at in the final part of this book.

For Further Reflection

1. Read Hebrews 12:4–14. According to this passage, what is the purpose of God's discipline on our lives?
2. Reread the story of the Pensacola revival at the start of the study. What special things do you notice about this revival? What led up to this revival and what results followed?
3. Look again at what happened in the Borneo revival of 1973. What did revival do to the worship of these people? (See Matthew 5:23–24.) List the main things you notice.
4. Some individuals or churches may get caught up with special experiences or the unusual things that happen in revival. But are these things the heart of true revival? What is?
5. According to Acts 2:41; 4:4; and 5:14, what was one of the results of the outpouring of the Holy Spirit upon the first disciples seen in the Acts of the Apostles?

6. Look again at the story of the Moravian revival. What does this example show are two important results of revival? How are the two connected?

7. You do not have to wait for revival before you seek holiness and become active in the harvest. You can begin now. What is God saying you can begin to do this week in the area of holiness and in the area of harvest?

PART 8

MAINTAINING
REVIVAL

I t is a wonderful thing to experience revival but quite another to maintain it. The fire of revival once started does not continue to burn automatically. History is full of examples of revivals that did not last. The Holy Spirit who comes sovereignly and powerfully is very sensitive and can just as easily withdraw His presence where there is sin, selfishness or disobedience. If we do not learn His ways and how to move with Him, the revival that began with such promise can quickly die.

In Part 8 of this book we will look at the three stages of revival, what causes revivals to die and how to maintain revival when it comes. We will also look at the importance of discipleship in conserving the fruit of revival.

21

THE THREE STAGES OF REVIVAL

> *God has chosen to bless his church with the full-*
> *ness of the Holy Spirit on the condition of its*
> *moving toward certain vital norms of health and*
> *witness.*
>
> Richard Lovelace, *Dynamics of Spiritual Life*

As we look at revivals of the past, we often see three main stages. Through these phases God's purpose is to bring His Church back to health and effective witness. If the Church will not go with what the Holy Spirit desires to do, then He will withdraw His presence and the revival will die. Let us look at each of these stages.

Time of Refreshing

The first stage of revival is when the Holy Spirit comes as rain upon the dry ground, a time of spiritual refreshing (see Acts 3:19). Mercy drops start to fall. It is a time of God's mercy and grace when He visits His people. We do not deserve it, nor have we earned it. Yet the Holy Spirit comes and begins moving and working in ways not seen before. There is excitement at the Holy Spirit's presence and activity. There is a new release of joy. There is new liberty. Times of worship come alive. The gifts of the Spirit are released. Miracles may happen. Certain phenomena may appear. There is excitement at what God is doing. God is moving among His people again.

During this phase of revival, God awakens us to who we are in Christ. We see the cross in a new way and realize how precious is the blood of Jesus that cleanses us from all sin. We experience His closeness. We see signs of His power. We come to realize that we are children of God and that He loves and accepts us unconditionally. But revival does not stay in this phase indefinitely—times of excitement and joy in sensing the Spirit's presence and power awaken new spiritual life in us. This phase of revival pulls the Church out of her rut, rouses her from sleep and sets her in motion. But through this phase of awakening and openness to His Spirit, Jesus is preparing us to move on to the second, more important, phase of revival.

Time of Discipline

In this second stage, God awakens us to who He is, which leads us into deeper repentance and cleansing. He now calls us to holiness, obedience and intimacy. This is a more difficult phase but is essential if the revival is to mature and last. God's purpose is to move us from spiritual childhood toward spiritual maturity. He wants to shift our attention from the gifts and "toys" He gives us (as signs of the Father's love), to the formation of character through training in holiness. He wants to establish us deeply in His Word to keep us from extremes and errors and to train us in right living (see 2 Timothy 3:17). His purpose is to mature us so that we seek Him for who He is rather than for what He gives us. God desires our fellowship. He wants us to draw near to Him and "walk in the light, as he is in the light" (1 John 1:7). He wants us to become like Him.

When revival first comes, certain things may be intensified in a way that may seem strange or abnormal. This is to awaken us again to what God is able to do. But as the revival matures, God leads us on into what He always expects to be present in our lives. The phenomena may pass away, but now obedience to Christ's call and the fruit of holy lives are important.

Revival must always lead us into holiness of life if it is to endure. The Holy Spirit is the *Spirit of holiness.* His main work is to lead us into holiness so that we can enjoy sweet fellowship with God (see Hebrews 12:14). This is why revival and holiness are always linked. God's chief concern is not to make us happy but to make us holy. He is more concerned with our character than our comfort. He is not just here to satisfy us physically but to perfect us spiritually. And this shaping of our character takes place through the disciplines of the Spirit. This means He will shake out of our lives and out of His Church all that is not centered on His Son—worldliness, idolatry, secret sins, human control, disunity. His purpose is to prepare Christ's Bride so that she will be holy, radiant, without spot or blemish and blameless at His coming (see Ephesians 5:26–27).

Many Christians do not like this part of revival. It is costly. It is humbling. It means confession and repentance. It is a time of purging and refining. It is a period of reformation and change. It means discipline and discipleship. But if the Church does not follow her Lord out of the first phase of revival into a restoration of holiness, then the revival will die and the move of God will dry up. The history of revival is full of examples of moves of God's Spirit that did not last and ended in disunity, false teaching, excesses and a falling away. While it is easy to receive the rich sense of joy from the Lord in the first phase of revival, it is more difficult to be disciplined as a son or daughter. Many Christians want to stay in the first phase of revival. To go on into holiness and deep heart repentance seems too costly. But we either go on or lose it—we cannot stand still.

Time of Harvest

This is the third stage of revival. If revival begins in the Church, it must end in the world. Revival must take us somewhere. Its purpose is not only to prepare us as the Bride of Christ but to move us out to obey Jesus' call to make disciples of all nations. Revival must always result in a healthy, strong Church that has an influence on the lives of unbelievers and on society. It must always bring God's people to the place of witness, mission and harvest. God brings revival not just for the enjoyment of His people but for the glory of His name and the extension of His Kingdom.

Once Christians are revived and purified, there will be a new concern for the Kingdom of God. There will be a fresh desire to share the message of God's love with others. Just as Isaiah responded to God's call with the words "Here am I. Send me!" so we will do the same after God's fire has cleansed us (see Isaiah 6:8). The focus of this third stage of revival will be on Jesus as King and Lord of the earth. There will be a fresh awakening to our divine calling and task—to take the message of Christ to the nations. We will have a new concern for the lost around us and for the unfinished task beyond our borders.

As revived Christians respond to this call, there will be a global harvest with thousands won daily into the Kingdom of God. This is already happening in many parts of the world. Imagine what will happen when the Church worldwide is revived, matured and brought into this third phase of revival! Then we will see a global harvest such as we have never seen before! If we keep revival to ourselves, it will die. But if we give it away through evangelism and mission, it will continue to burn and spread.

For Further Reflection

1. Read Hebrews 12:7–15, 25–29.
2. Time of refreshing: What are the main marks of this first phase of revival? Why does God send times of refreshing? What is His purpose in this?
3. Time of discipline: What are the main marks of this second phase of revival? What is God's purpose in this

time of discipline according to Hebrews 6:1–2; 12:10–11, 14–15, 25–29?

4. If Christians experiencing revival do not respond to God's call to holiness and discipleship, what will happen?

5. Think again on the quote by Richard Lovelace at the start of this chapter. God has chosen to bless His Church with the fullness of the Holy Spirit on what conditions? What does this mean for your church and for you personally?

6. What has God been saying to you personally through this chapter? What practical steps can you begin to take this week to live in obedience to God's call?

22

WHY REVIVALS DIE

It is one thing to get revival, but quite another thing to keep it.

John Wesley, *Journals of John Wesley*

Sadly, the history of revival is full of examples of moves of God's Spirit that began powerfully but faded out in the end. Why is this? If revival comes sovereignly from the hand of God, then revival also dies because God has withdrawn His Spirit because of something we have failed to do. What causes revivals to die?

Neglect of Revival Principles

Revival comes as a result of obeying certain divine principles, which, as we have seen, are outlined in 2 Chronicles 7:14. If we humble ourselves, pray, seek God's face and turn from our wicked ways, He will come among us in revival blessing. But these same principles that prepare the way for revival also sustain revival once it comes. If, however, we become careless and neglect these principles, revival will die. If pride enters, or we pull back on prayer, neglect intimacy with God or fail to keep our hearts pure, God's Spirit will be grieved and His presence will be withdrawn. This may not happen suddenly. Just as a car running out of gas gradually slows down, so the initial momentum of revival may continue for some time after the presence of God's Spirit has gone. But there will be a gradual decline, and it may be a while before God's people realize that "the glory has departed" (1 Samuel 4:21).

Failure to Move on to Maturity

We have already looked at this in the last chapter. God's purpose is to move us from stage one, the time of refreshing, into stage two, the time of discipline, and then into stage three, the time of harvest. But if Christians do not want to move on toward maturity, the revival will dry up. If Christians think that revival has to do only with the excitement, spiritual phenomena and manifestations seen in the time of refreshing, and do not progress toward spiritual health and outward witness, the Holy Spirit will eventually withdraw His presence. This will result in spiritual decline and a return to where we were before the revival began.

Opposition from Satan

In the book of Acts we see that any advance of the Kingdom of God was met with a direct counterattack from Satan. This may come externally through opposition and persecution. Or it may come from within through disunity or other problems. In the 1970s a revival began in the Sepik district of Papua New Guinea. But after starting strongly, it eventually died away because of a strong demonic backlash. In one church in particular, the power of evil gained an entrance and there were serious excesses. Three discouraging years went by, and the Christians felt hopeless and powerless against the cults and darkness of sin. Revival means intense spiritual warfare. Where Christians are not alert, or do not know how to stand against the attacks of the devil, they will easily be overcome and the move of God will be spoiled.

Richard Lovelace gives the following summary of five main ways Satan attacks revivals:[1]

1. Attack directly with despair or discouragement.
2. Plant lies, rumors and false pictures in the minds of unbelievers or unrevived Christians so that they will reject the work of God and attack its progress.
3. Set the leaders against each other and so divide and conquer.
4. Get the converts to go to extremes and so discredit the movement.
5. Produce counterfeit miracles to discredit the real ones.

Lack of Christlike Humility and Love

Jonathan Edwards believed that pride is the biggest thing that kills revivals. Pride is such a subtle trap because it often snares those who are most eager to promote revival. They can become proud of the revival that has come to them or their church and take the glory for themselves. But God will not give His glory to another (see Isaiah 42:8). Continuous revival can only thrive in an atmosphere of Christlike humility and love. When feelings of superiority, pride or personal glory come in, the glory of God departs.

Disunity

I remember in 1991 ministering in a church in the Solomon Islands that had experienced revival. During the convention meetings, it became clear that the Holy Spirit was not moving as He had before. Something was wrong. After the close of one of the meetings, one of the elders got up and confessed that the reason was lack of unity among the leadership. Just a week before in one of their leadership meetings, there had been disagreement and angry feelings toward each other, which had remained unresolved. So now during the convention meetings, the Holy Spirit had withdrawn His presence. This elder called all the other leaders together after the meeting to sort out the problem, which they did, staying up late into the night until differences were dealt with and unity restored. The next morning, when we gathered for our final service, the presence of God returned and the Spirit of God moved powerfully. Many responded outwardly to the Word of God, and the meeting went on for over five hours! Nobody wanted to leave.

The Holy Spirit is the Spirit of unity. Where Christians are bound together in love and unity, there God will command His blessing (see Psalm 133). It is in an atmosphere of love, acceptance and forgiveness that the Holy Spirit works. But where there is disunity (and especially at the leadership level), the Holy Spirit is grieved and withdraws His influence. Where there are barriers between believers, the Holy Spirit cannot flow. And if disunity remains without being dealt with, the revival will quickly die.

Human Control

Revivals start with a sovereign work of the Holy Spirit who takes control of His Church and moves the way He chooses. Revivals die when people take control again and try to predict, program or direct the Spirit to work the way they want Him to work. Churches that have lost revival may try hard to maintain its outward forms, but without the presence of God this leads only to heaviness and human striving. The result is legalism—living by rules and formulas rather than by the leadership, liberty and power of the Spirit.

161

Lack of Bible Teaching and Discipleship

Revival brings both fire and wind. But the fuel, as we have seen, that keeps the fire burning is the Word of God. Without fresh fuel any fire will die down and go out. The same wind that causes a fire to burn strongly at the start will cause a fire to burn out if no fresh fuel is added. Moves of God that have relied on the excitement of the Spirit's activity, but have not built the people in the Word of God, have soon burned out. It is said of the Welsh revival that its impact was not as lasting as it should have been because of a lack of Bible teaching. Revivals that have not taught the Word of God or led the people into the disciplines of discipleship have not lasted.

Lack of Outward Mission Concern

Jonathan Edwards, a key person in the First Great Awakening in America, believed that for revival to continue there must be a balance between personal concern for individuals and social concern. He believed that concern only for the spiritual lives of believers in the form of meetings, prayer, singing and "religious talk" would not promote or sustain revival. There had to be outward works of love and mercy reaching into the community and beyond into mission activity. We are not meant to be a reservoir but a *river*. God's Spirit is not just given to fill us up but to flow through us. God brings revival not just for our enjoyment but for the glory of His name and the extension of His Kingdom. Whenever the Holy Spirit filled the first disciples, it was always for the purpose of proclamation and mission (see Acts 2:4–12; 4:8–10, 31). Where that has not happened in revivals of the past, the end has often been confusion and disappointment, and the revival has dried up.

162

Generation Gap

Revival may decline because of a rising generation that has not experienced it personally (see Judges 2:7, 10). Unless they also catch the fire, the revival will die. Revival does not pass automatically to the new generation. As with conversion, each generation must meet God personally and encounter Him anew. Fresh fire is needed to ignite the hearts of the young. Older believers must be careful to pour their lives into the youth, teaching them the principles they have learned, becoming mentors and models for them and then praying that they, too, will catch the fire.

For Further Reflection

1. Read Hebrews 2:1–4; 3:7–15. What do these verses say to you about how to avoid spiritual decline? What must you be careful to do (or not to do)?
2. We have looked at nine reasons why revivals die. Select two of these that have spoken to you most clearly. What are they saying to you?
3. Richard Lovelace suggests five main ways Satan attacks revival. Have you seen any of these happening in "revivals" you know? Which ones?
4. Disunity: Look again at the example from the Solomon Islands. What important lessons come from this?
5. Generation gap: Read Judges 2:7, 10. What reason is given here for spiritual decline after a time of "revival"? What can you do to help pass on the fire of love for Jesus to the rising generation? (If you are a parent, see Deuteronomy 6:4–9.)
6. What practical steps can you take to make sure you keep growing in a closer relationship with Jesus? What is God saying to you through this chapter?

23

REVIVAL AND DISCIPLESHIP

In order to preserve the fruit of revival and transform society, the church must move beyond making converts and give its attention to bringing converts to maturity.

Mark Shaw, *Ten Great Ideas from Church History*

During the ministry of John Wesley, there was a revival in England with many new converts brought into the Kingdom of God. But what happened to these converts and those Christians awakened by revival? Were they left to find their own way? Did John Wesley just hope they would know how to grow into strong disciples of Jesus on their own? No! Wesley had a plan. Those touched by revival were joined into small discipleship groups of around twelve people (called "societies"). Over each group Wesley appointed laypersons as spiritual guides responsible for looking after these small flocks. In these groups the members regularly met together and joined in prayer and singing, confessed their sins to one another, shared Christian experiences through testimony, were taught the Word of God and received spiritual support and encouragement. This gave the revival strength and made the results long lasting.

John Wesley's Secret

Wesley's idea was a simple one: The Church changes the world not by making converts but by making disciples.[1] The method he used was small discipleship groups. This had a great impact in conserving the fruit of revival long after the initial fires of revival had passed. And because Wesley's followers used this same "method" of small-group training, they later became known as "Methodists."

What was the result of this plan? By the end of John Wesley's life, he had 79,000 followers in Britain and 40,000 in America. When Wesley died, he left behind few material possessions but a spiritual legacy that has changed the world. It is recorded that all he left was a worn-out preacher's Bible, a coat, a library of books and something else—the Methodist Church!

The Testimony of George Whitefield

George Whitefield was a great revival preacher at the same time as Wesley. He preached with passion and fire and saw thousands of converts under his ministry. But he had no discipling plan like Wesley. Toward the end of his ministry, he made this confession:

> My brother Wesley acted wisely. The souls that were awakened under his ministry he joined in classes [small groups] and thus preserved the fruits of his labors. This I neglected and my people are a rope of sand.[2]

A rope of sand has neither strength nor cohesion because it is made of individual grains not bound together. The results of Whitefield's ministry could not easily be traced. His converts had dissolved as a group and scattered.

Revival and discipleship must go together. Revival brings the wind and the fire. Discipleship provides the wood and

165

keeps the fire stoked and burning. But if there is no wood, what happens? It is like a grass fire that flares up momentarily and then burns out, leaving only ashes behind. But if the wood of the Word is put on the fire, and the revived believers are trained in discipleship, the fire continues to burn and spread.

Those renewed by the Spirit in revival need to be taught the Word of God and trained in discipleship as an ongoing way of life. Only in this way will revival be conserved. But we do not need to wait for revival to come to start this process. Jesus' final command to His followers was to "go and make disciples" (Matthew 28:19). This is more than just winning converts; it means winning converts and then bringing them to spiritual maturity. Discipleship training, then, should be the Church's priority at all times. The Church needs to be committed to making disciples as its central activity. Then, when revival comes, we will know how to conserve the results.

Solomon Islands Revival

George Strachan, a missionary with the South Seas Evangelical Church in the Solomon Islands, believes that it was the in-depth teaching of the Word of God that prepared the South Seas Evangelical Church for revival in 1970 and kept the fires burning long afterwards. He says:

> From its beginning the church had been steeped in God's Word. The vital place of the Bible in the life of the Christian has been stressed through to the present day. Early missionaries concentrated on producing simple Bible literature. . . . These studies laid a firm foundation for the church. When revival came national leaders were able to give a strong scriptural lead. This has largely accounted for the continuance of the movement.[3]

Prepare for the Harvest!

Across the world today we see the beginnings of a global harvest of people being won into the Kingdom of God. The fires of revival are burning in many places. But are we ready for a mighty harvest in our nation? What will a church do when revival comes and awakens Christians with a deep hunger for the Word of God? What will we do when new converts come flooding in? Those churches that already have discipleship training in place will know how to take these believers on to maturity. But unprepared churches will be overwhelmed and unable to cope. As a result, they will largely miss out on what God wants to do. God will not give us a share in the harvest if we are not prepared for it. He will not entrust a flood of new converts to our care if we do not know how to nurture them. However, when the fire of revival comes, those churches already doing what He has called them to do will not only catch the fire but will be able to keep it burning strongly and make it long lasting.

Because of this urgent need to know how to make disciples, I have prepared a discipleship training series to help churches and individuals get back to this primary task. (See details at the end of this book.) This training series will provide you with simple, clear tools to help you in the task of turning "seekers" into believers, believers into disciples and disciples into disciple-makers. It will help you become a strong disciple of Jesus yourself and then show you how to disciple others. Begin preparing now!

For Further Reflection

1. Read Hebrews 5:11–14; 6:1–3. What was the problem with these Hebrew Christians? How much do you think these words in Hebrews 5:11–14 still describe many

Christians today? (Think about your own church.) How much do they apply to you?

2. Think about the story of John Wesley at the start of the chapter. What purpose do you think he had in forming these small discipleship groups and what effect did they have on the revival at that time?

3. In your own spiritual development were you ever discipled like this? If so, to what extent? And how did it help you in your Christian life? (If not, how could it have helped you?)

4. In contrast to Wesley, what do you think Whitefield meant by saying that his people were "a rope of sand"? What benefit did he see in the way Wesley discipled his converts?

5. Think about Mark Shaw's quote at the start of the chapter. What do these words say to you about the importance of discipleship in your own life and in the life of your church? Is there anything you can do about it now?

PART 9

A PEOPLE PREPARED

We come now to the final section of this book. How can we be a people prepared for the Lord? Luke 1:17 is a key verse. It speaks of what John the Baptist had to do to prepare the way for the Messiah.

> And he will go on before the Lord, in the spirit and power of Elijah, to turn the hearts of the fathers to their children and the disobedient to the wisdom of the righteous—to make ready a people prepared for the Lord.
>
> Luke 1:17

God longs to send revival to His Church, to make her a glorious, radiant Church without spot or wrinkle at His coming. But He needs a people who are prepared. Perhaps the same preparations are needed today as in John the Baptist's time.

There needs to be renewal in the home, and there needs to be a return to holy living if we are to be a people prepared for the Lord.

Revival is not a miraculous visitation of God falling upon an unprepared and unwilling people. God sends revival when His people earnestly seek Him and are ready for His coming. Do you want revival? Is your heart prepared? In these final three chapters we will look at how to be a people prepared for the Lord.

24

PREPARATION BEGINS AT HOME!

Revival comes when Christians are longing for
God, and God alone.

Brian Edwards, *Revival*

Richard Baxter, a great preacher and writer, lived in England in the seventeenth century (1615–91). At one time he became pastor of a church in a very difficult town. For three years he preached with all the passion of his heart, but with little response. One day in desperation he threw himself down on the floor of his study and cried out, "Lord, why don't You do something with these people? I can't go on! If You don't do something, I'll die!" At that moment, Baxter said, it was as if he heard a voice speaking back to him, *Baxter, you're working in the wrong place. You're expecting revival to come through the church. Try the home!*[1]

This caused Richard Baxter to change his whole approach to ministry. He began visiting the homes of his members one by one. He would spend whole evenings with them encouraging them to have personal and family devotions and showing parents how to set up a time of family worship with their children. Gradually the Spirit of God began to light fires of renewal in homes across his parish. It was not long before these fires swept through his whole church and revival came. The church became powerful and "Richard Baxter" a famous name.

Many Christians want revival today. They are waiting for it to start in the Church. But perhaps God is saying the same thing He said to Richard Baxter: "You're looking in the wrong place. You're expecting revival to come through the Church. Try the home!" Preparing for revival begins in our hearts and homes. It is there God first wants to meet with you. Then, as He begins to bring renewal there, He will bring revival to our churches and finally to our land.

Prepare Your Own Heart

God is looking for a people who are prepared, and that preparation begins with you in the quietness of your own heart. We have looked at what this means through the studies of this book. Prepare for revival in the secret place, in your times alone with God. Ask God to revive *you* first of all. Seek Him with all your heart (see Jeremiah 29:13). Spend time each day in His presence. Open your heart to Him in adoration and worship. Seek His face. Pour out your heart before Him in prayer. Long to know Him more intimately through His Word. Let Him be your awakening thought and closing prayer. Let Him touch the deep levels of your life and change you. Humble yourself before Him and let Him deal with the hard, resistant areas of your life and the pride that lurks within. Revival is always personal before it is public. It cannot come to the Church without first touching the hearts of individual believers. Prepare your own heart to catch the fire when revival comes. That is where revival begins.

Prepare Your Own Home

Then ask God to bring renewal to your family relationships. Ask Him to give you a new love for your wife, your husband,

172

your children, your parents, your brothers and sisters and your wider family. Live in humility with each other. Say "sorry" and seek forgiveness where that is needed. Live with compassion and kindness toward each other. As marriage partners, live the way God has called you to live (see Ephesians 5:21–33). Family life has to be changed before society can be changed. The Christian home should be the model of what happy, healthy relationships should be when Christ is at the center. That's why we desperately need revival to start there. How can you expect to experience revival without it changing the way you live at home?

If you are a parent, realize that your ministry begins at home with your children before it extends anywhere else. If you neglect your home responsibilities, no one can take your place. Teach your children by word and example how to love the Lord. Model the Christian life before them. As you love the Lord with all your heart, teach them by word and example to do the same (see Deuteronomy 6:4–9). Values are caught more than taught. Discipling begins at home with your children. Let your children see that your devotion and obedience to Christ is the most important thing in your life.

Fathers! Reconnect with Your Children

A key area in preparing for revival is restoring the relationship between fathers and children. This was John the Baptist's main ministry in preparing for the coming of Jesus. He was called "to turn the hearts of the fathers to their children" (Luke 1:17). This was to be the primary task of the forerunner of the Lord (see Malachi 4:6). Many fathers are not close to their children. They are so busy with work, outside interests and even church ministry that they have little meaningful time with them. But to be a people prepared for the Lord, fathers are the key. They must turn their hearts toward their children and fulfill their God-given responsibilities at home.

Fathers, you are meant to be the family priest representing your family before God. Do not leave the spiritual welfare of your children to your wife, your church or a Christian school. You are responsible to be the spiritual head of your family and to give the lead. Take time to build close relationships with your wife and children. As you love your wife, so God's love will flow into your home. Read Bible stories to your children and pray with them. Worship and pray together as a family. Train and discipline your children with love and gentleness rather than severity and harshness. The picture your children get of their heavenly Father is strongly influenced by the picture they have of you! Play with your children, share in their lives, do things together and be there for them. God is looking for godly fathers (and mothers) who will turn their hearts to their children and take time to love, discipline and train them in the ways of the Lord (see Ephesians 6:4). Are you willing to make this your priority? A people prepared for the Lord begins at home. Are you ready to start there?

The Person God Uses

Don't wait for revival to begin in the Church. Let it begin with you! God is looking for a people prepared. He is looking for those who have hearts and homes ready to catch the fire. And He is looking for those who will be the spark that sets the fire off. If you are prepared, He could use you. No one can be used in revival who has not been revived first. God can use ordinary people to do extraordinary things. All He requires is hearts totally committed to Him (see 2 Chronicles 16:9). He is looking for those who are "humble and contrite in spirit" and who "tremble" at His Word (see Isaiah 66:2). These are the kinds of people God used in the past—ordinary people like Nicholas von Zinzendorf, Jonathan Edwards, John and Charles Wesley, Evan Roberts and many others right up to today. They were not all gifted, highly educated or mighty, but they had a longing for God and a commitment to prayer and God used them. He can do the same with you! Today we need people like them who have a passion for God and God alone. Don't just wait with folded arms and think there is nothing you can do. God wants to use you. Will you be a part of what He is doing? Then begin to get ready now!

For Further Reflection

1. Read Malachi 4:6; Luke 1:11–17.
2. Look again at the story of Richard Baxter at the start of the chapter. What was the key thing that prepared the way for revival to come to his church? What is this story saying to you about the way to prepare for revival? Where should you begin?
3. Prepare your own heart: Reread this section in the chapter. What do you need to do in order to prepare your own heart for revival? What is God saying to you?
4. Prepare your own home: Reread this section. If you are married, how should you be living at home, according to the following references? Deuteronomy 6:4–9; Ephesians 5:21–33; 6:1–3. Are you living like that?
5. Fathers! Reconnect with your children: What does it mean for you as a father (or parent) to "turn your heart toward your children"? And what does it mean as a son or daughter to "turn your heart toward your father (or parents)"? How can you do this? (See Ephesians 6:1–4.)
6. The person God uses: Reread this section in the chapter. According to the following references, what is the kind of person God uses? (See 2 Chronicles 16:9; Isaiah 66:2; 1 Corinthians 1:26–29.)
7. What is God saying to you personally through this chapter? What do you need to do in order to be a person prepared for the Lord? Where can you start this week?

25

THE POWER OF UNITY

*When churches in a region come together in prayer
and in visible unity, something happens in the
heavenly places that breaks Satan's power over the
Church and eventually over that region.*

Ed Silvoso, *That None Should Perish*

How can we be a people prepared for the Lord? In the last chapter we looked at where to begin. We begin by preparing our own hearts and our own homes. But it does not stop there. The next important preparation is within the family of God. Jesus prayed that we might be one as He and the Father are one so that the world might believe (see John 17:21). When God's people come together in visible love and unity, He begins to work in amazing ways. Let's see what this means in practice.

A Story from Colombia

Before 1995, the city of Cali in Colombia, South America, was known as the drug capital of the world. Drug lords with deep roots in the occult ruled the city. For years Colombia was the biggest exporter of cocaine in the world. Drug trafficking controlled every part of society. There were violence and corruption everywhere. It was dangerous to walk the streets, and there was a satanic darkness over the city. People were ruled by fear and were powerless to do anything about it.

The churches were weak and struggling and worked independently of each other. There was no coming together. But that soon changed. It began when a group of pastors from different churches began confessing their wrong attitudes toward one another and seeking forgiveness and reconciliation. Then God began to reveal that until His people from all the churches came together in united prayer, there would be no hope for this city. Individual churches and Christians were praying, but not until the call went out in 1995 for churches to unite visibly in prayer did things begin to change. Much to the surprise of everyone, thousands of Christians came out that first night to pray through the night in an open-air soccer stadium. The enemy struck back, and one of the organizing pastors was shot and killed. This tragedy shocked the Christian community but led to a deeper and greater unity of the pastors of the city. Soon all-night "prayer vigils" were held each month, with more than sixty thousand Christians from across the churches gathering to pray together in the largest stadium in the city. There they worshiped and prayed for the breaking of satanic strongholds over their city.

The results were almost immediate. Corruption dropped dramatically. The number of murders decreased. Drug lords were arrested and their power broken. Prominent citizens in the city became Christians. The spiritual atmosphere of the city began to change. There was a new openness to the Gospel. Christians found a new freedom and confidence to speak about Christ everywhere and people were hungry to hear more. Churches began to experience explosive growth. Without any special strategies, churches were growing faster than they could manage. One church swelled to 35,000 and began holding seven services every Sunday. Almost every church in Cali was now growing!

What caused such a dramatic change in this evil city? Church leaders in Cali know this is a miracle of God that has come in response to their unity and fervent prayer. It is a process that continues with repentance and reconciliation uniting Christians and sweeping away barriers to evangelism. God chose a city like Cali to demonstrate what He can do in any city or nation when churches repent, come together in love and unity and pray. That is where God commands His blessing. If God can do that in a city like Cali, He can do it anywhere.[1]

Stories from Past Revivals

This story from Colombia is not new. It has happened throughout history. And it is happening today in countries such as Brazil and Argentina, among others. Whenever God's people have humbled themselves, repented of their pride and disunity, put aside their differences and come together in united prayer, God has worked in amazing ways.

It happened in America. The Second Great Awakening began as a result of a call in 1794 for pastors of every denomination in the United States to join together to pray for revival. Conditions were at their worst and churches knew they were in great need, so pastors and people responded. Soon America was covered with a network of prayer meetings, where Christians prayed for revival on the first Monday of each month. And out of that united prayer a great revival came—the Second Great Awakening.

More than sixty years later, in 1857, when conditions had run down and the country was seriously divided over the issue of slavery, a man of prayer, a layman, Jeremiah Lanphier, started a businessmen's lunchtime prayer meeting in an upper room in Manhattan, New York. In response to his invitations, only six people came out of a population of more than a million. But the following week there were 14 and the next week 23. Then it was decided to meet every day for prayer. Within four months every church and hall in downtown New York was filled with people of every church denomination gathering to pray. A newspaper reporter was sent around the prayer meetings to see how many were praying. In one hour he could get to twelve meetings only but counted more than six thousand people!

Then a landslide of prayer began, which overflowed into the churches. People began to be converted—ten thousand a week in New York City alone. The movement spread, and people began gathering in churches to pray at eight in the morning, twelve noon and six in the evening. And out of that united prayer another great revival swept across America, with more than a million converted in the first year. This revival then jumped across the Atlantic to Ireland, Scotland, Wales, England and other parts of the world.[2]

Where God Commands His Blessing

What God has done in the past, and what He is doing today in other parts of the world, He can do where you are. All He is waiting for is a people prepared—prepared in heart and prepared to come together in unity to pray and seek His face.

The three deadliest strongholds that undermine the mission of the Church in a city or region are disunity, spiritual apathy and ignorance of the schemes of the devil. But when churches in a region come together in prayer and in visible unity, something happens in the heavenly places that breaks Satan's power over the Church and eventually over that region. God then begins to work in powerful ways.

Perfect unity will not be possible this side of heaven. But despite our surface differences, we are called to recognize and preserve the unity of the Spirit that already exists (see Ephesians 4:3). How do we do that? Unity within an individual church is important. But if Satan's strongholds across a city or a nation are to be broken, unity among the churches is essential. God commands His blessing and releases His power only as far as that unity exists. If unity is within one church, His blessing will rest there. But if God is to touch a whole city or nation, unity must extend between the churches so that His blessing and power can flow into that region. If this is to happen, steps to unity have to begin at the leadership level of the churches. But how can that be possible? Here are some keys.[3]

Steps to unity:

1. Pastors (and congregations) in a region should see themselves as equal members of the same team with Jesus as the head Coach, rather than working in isolation and even in competition with each other.
2. Pastors can begin to break down barriers by going to other pastors and humbling themselves first of all. This means confessing their lack of concern for each other, their spirit of pride, their independence and even their opposition to each other.
3. Pastors should then begin praying together as pastors in a region. If not all pastors will join in, pray with those who will. Focus on what you have in common in Christ rather than on your differences.
4. Begin as a church to pray for other pastors and their churches. One pastor in Argentina began praying for different pastors and their congregations every Sunday in his church service, and this resulted in dramatic reconciliations between formerly unfriendly congregations.
5. Show practical demonstrations of care and support for other churches. For example, one pastor who knew another church was struggling to raise enough money for their new church building called his congregation to take up a special offering for them.
6. See your church as only one small part of Christ's greater Church across your city or region. In Stockton, California, the pastors and their congregations agreed that whenever they talked to non-Christians they would introduce themselves as pastors and people of the Church in that city, purposely avoiding any reference to their own denominations. Now nonbelievers are beginning to use the same expression—the Church in the city—rather than denominational or individual names.

7. Celebrations of unity—where pastors of one denomination are invited to speak in churches of another denomination, and where church congregations in a region unite together for prayer, public rallies and special occasions.

Where God's people are prepared in heart to work together in unity, there is no limit to what God can do. There God will command His blessing and reveal His glory.

For Further Reflection

1. Read Psalm 133:1–3; John 17:20–24.
2. Reread the story from Colombia at the beginning of the chapter. What impresses you most about this story? What do you see as the main keys that brought about this amazing change in the city of Cali?
3. Reread the stories of past revivals in America. What important lessons come out of these stories?
4. Why is unity among Christians so important, according to Psalm 133; John 13:34–45; 17:20–23; Ephesians 4:1–5?
5. Does unity among Christians mean there must be uniformity (all exactly the same in doctrine, style of worship, church government, etc.)? What does it mean? (See 1 Corinthians 12:12–26.)
6. Where God commands His blessing: Reread this section and think again about the quote at the start of the chapter. If God is to release His blessing and power across a city or region, what has to happen?
7. Steps to unity: Look again at the steps to unity Ed Silvoso has seen at work in the revival in Argentina (last section of the chapter). Tick the ones that you have seen happening among churches in your area.
8. What can you do yourself to deepen unity within your own church and between Christians of other churches? Write down any steps you can take.

26

"LORD, DO IT AGAIN!"

Everything God has told us to do we ought to do,
but having done it all, we must still wait upon
Him to do what He alone can do.

Richard Owen Roberts, *Revival*

The story is told of a group of Christian leaders visiting England who were taken on a tour to visit the cottage where John Wesley had lived so many years before. They saw the cottage still preserved as it was in Wesley's time. They were reminded of the great revival that began through Wesley's ministry, a revival that transformed England and touched the world. The team passed the bedroom and saw the place where Wesley had knelt beside his bed to pray—grooves were worn in the wooden floor from the many times he had prayed there! As they left the cottage and boarded their bus, someone noticed one of the team members was not with them. When they went back to find where he was, they found him in John Wesley's bedroom kneeling beside his bed, with his knees in the same grooves, crying out, "Lord, do it again! Do it again!"

Winkie Pratney says, "Christians who do learn from revival history will be compelled to want to repeat it."[1] Is that true of you too? Does the record of God's mighty deeds in the past make you stand in awe of Him? And does it create a longing in your heart to see God do in our time what He has done before?

Most Christians will listen to stories of revival with interest. Some will pray occasionally for revival. Others will talk about the great acts of God in revival. But often only a few have a deep longing for revival, whatever the cost and however long it takes, and are willing to get down on their knees to pray. What the Church needs today is Christians who have a hunger and longing for revival, hundreds of thousands of them, who are willing to prepare their hearts and pay the price for revival, people who will give themselves no rest till revival comes. Are you willing to be one of these?

Healing for the Land

Our nation and the nations of the world desperately need to return to God. Throughout the pages of this book, we have seen that God's people are the key to this happening. It must start with us. God has promised:

> If my people, who are called by my name, will humble them-selves and pray and seek my face and turn from their wicked ways, then will I hear from heaven and will forgive their sin and will heal their land.
>
> 2 Chronicles 7:14

Revival as God intends does not just bring new life to His Church; it should spill over into the world and bring healing to the nations.

Revivals of the past have not only changed the Church but have been used by God to bring healing to the social, moral and spiritual lives of nations. Revival has healed racial tensions, brought reconciliation to opposing parties, changed the hearts of men toward women, changed the hearts of fathers to their children, healed divided families, brought love into marriage and family life, reduced alcoholism and crime and changed society for the better. When God revives His Church and makes her healthy, strong and attractive, the influence will be felt at all levels of social life. God's people become again like salt and light in the nation. Their influence stops moral rot and brings light and hope to people in spiritual darkness and despair. Isn't that why we desperately need revival in our land? Well, that is what God is longing to bring.

In the Meantime, What Should We Do?

Revival is a sovereign move of God. But does this mean we just sit down and wait with folded arms for revival to come when He chooses to send it? Second Chronicles 7:14 has made it clear that there is something we should do and must do; there are steps we must take and preparations we must make before the Lord will come in revival blessing. We have seen what these things are through the chapters of this book and how to prepare the way: We need to repent of our pride. We need to join together as the Body of Christ to pray and seek God's face as we have never sought Him before. "Revival comes when Christians are longing for God, and God alone."[2] And the story of revival history shows us that.

But there is something further we should do. We should set our hearts toward those things that are the result of revival. The results of revival are a fresh desire for prayer, worship, intimacy with God, discipleship, dependence on the Holy Spirit, unity and compassion for the lost. These are what God expects to be present in the life of His Church normally, and we should seek them. This is what vibrant New Testament Christianity is all about. Don't be satisfied with the way things are now. Whatever we find in true revival, long for these things. And as we faithfully devote ourselves to what God has called us to do, we must then wait on Him to do what only He can do. Remember, revival will not come by simply copying the results of revivals elsewhere. Revival is a sovereign act of God beyond human control. We cannot achieve by our own efforts what God alone by His Holy Spirit can do. But God expects us to seek His face first and then to seek His righteousness. He expects us to be constantly doing those things He has called us to do. Then, when the time is right, He will take up these things in greater measure when He pours out His Spirit upon us.

Time to Get Ready!

In times of drought, we must still water gardens and fields with hoses and pumps to keep them green and to produce crops. This takes great effort and expense. Yet we must still do it. It is no use just folding our arms and doing nothing in the hope that the rains will come. We must do what we can now. The result is little patches of green on a very dry landscape.

But when the rains from heaven come, whole regions are soaked in a few hours, the countryside turns green within a day or two and abundant crops follow. How easy it is to bring in a harvest when God sends the rain at the right time! Rain from heaven is so much better than water from earth. How easy it is for God and how hard for us. God will do it sovereignly, but He wants us to be ready with the fields of our hearts plowed soft and deep and the seed already sown. And He expects us faithfully to water the small patch of ground He has given to our care. Then, when the time is right, He will do what only He can do—He will send revival rains. Will you be ready when His Spirit comes upon the thirsty ground?

Gipsy Smith was once asked how to start a revival. He answered:

> Go home, lock yourself in your room, kneel down in the middle of your floor. Draw a chalk mark all around yourself and ask God to start the revival inside that chalk mark. When he has answered your prayer, the revival will be on.[3]

That is where revival begins. Why don't you stop and do that right now and ask God to begin revival in you!

For Further Reflection

1. As we read about revivals of the past, this can create a longing within our hearts: "Oh, Lord, do it again! Do in our day what You have done before!" Is this how you feel? How does the story at the start of the chapter speak to you?
2. Read the longing expressed by Isaiah (64:1–5) and Habakkuk (3:1–2). Then express in your own words how you feel. Write this as a prayer to God.
3. Healing for the land: What do you think 2 Chronicles 7:14 means when it talks about "healing the land"? What kinds of healing are spoken about in the following references? 2 Corinthians 5:18–20; Malachi 2:13–16; 4:5–6; Ephesians 2:14–16. What kinds of healing do you think we need in our land?
4. Think about the quotation of Richard Owen Roberts at the start of the chapter. What do you think he means? List some of these things we should be doing now. (See the second section in the chapter.)
5. After completing the chapters of this book, what parts have spoken to you most clearly? What changes have you already experienced and what do you need to do further to "prepare the way for the Lord"?

A FINAL WORD

If you have completed the chapters and reflection questions in this book, congratulations! I trust this has opened your understanding to what revival is and had a positive impact on your life by helping you prepare the way for the Lord.

But this is not the end for you; it is only the beginning of what you are now to do as an ongoing way of life. Don't be just a hearer but a *doer* of the Word. Continue to apply the principles you have learned from 2 Chronicles 7:14. Review the chapters of this book regularly. This will keep your heart soft and open to the Holy Spirit's working in your life. Then use this book to help others in the same way. God is looking for a people prepared. As you prepare your own heart, you may find opportunities to help others prepare their hearts also.

Remember that discipleship and revival go together (see chapter 23 in this book). So if you have not yet worked through the discipleship training series outlined on page 199, you might consider this as the next stage of your spiritual journey in preparing the way for the Lord.

May you be one of this present generation who seeks God's face and may He find in you one prepared to be a part of all He wants to do in our time.

Postscript

A Personal Testimony

It was Easter 1989. I was with a team of eight other pastors from Australia visiting the Solomon Islands—a cluster of islands in the South Pacific where revival had been burning for many years. We were there to experience revival firsthand and see for ourselves what God was doing.

It was the final meeting of an Easter convention on the island of Malaita. More than a thousand people were packed into the small village church. God had already been working powerfully during the three days leading up to this final meeting, bringing the people to repentance. Michael Maeliau, a Solomon Island leader of the South Seas Evangelical Church, was the speaker.

As this final meeting came to a close with worship and prayer, we were encouraged to make our own inward response to God. Michael Maeliau called us to offer ourselves afresh to the Lord as a living sacrifice. Then he invited us all to pray, and, typical of the way the Solomon Island people pray, everyone began to pray out loud simultaneously so that the church was filled with the noise of more than a thousand voices raised in prayer.

A Powerful Visitation

Within a few moments an incredible thing happened. I could hear from the back of the church a loud sound above the noise of people praying, and it gradually moved forward over the congregation like a great wave. Everyone present would have heard it. As this wave of sound touched people, the intensity of their praying increased—which added to the sound's volume. The noise was like the roar of a mighty waterfall (or was it the sound of a mighty rushing wind like at Pentecost?). It continued to move forward from the back of the church. I could hear it coming closer and closer to where I was sitting with the other Australian pastors, just a few rows from the front. Then, for a moment, it seemed to hover right over us like a mighty wave about to break, and then it fell and rolled over me and those around me like a huge breaker.

At that instant I was engulfed by a warm sensation that flowed all over me, and a deep cry and groan was released from deep within. I began to cry and sob uncontrollably. The volume of voices around me was now at a deafening pitch as those around me were inundated by the wave. For about twenty minutes I was caught up with God and cried uncontrollably as the Holy Spirit powerfully touched my life. My own crying and sobbing were inaudible because of the noise around me; God was dealing with other people as well. I believe now that His work in me was to bring a profound release within that I had never experienced before. God was releasing me from emotions, conflicts and hurts I had bottled up for years, and He was now washing me clean and setting me free. I saw no vision as others did, there was no conviction of sin or failure (though there was for others), no images of anything came into my mind and I didn't even know why I was crying—except that I knew God was doing something deep in my life that I did not fully understand and that I could not control. All I knew was that this was the Holy Spirit at work in a way I had never experienced before. Truly, this was a divine visitation, and the Holy Spirit was awesomely present among us.

God Dealing Personally

This outpouring of the Spirit probably lasted half an hour. The whole meeting during this time was out of human control. No one tried to interfere or direct what was happening. God was visiting His people and the speaker, Michael Maeliau, stood back and let the Holy Spirit take over and do what He wanted to do. During the time God was dealing with me, I was unaware of what was happening to others all around me. I had no idea how the other members of the Australian team were being affected but supposed that they too were experiencing what I was experiencing. Later, however, after it was all over, we talked about it and shared what each had experienced. I was surprised to discover that the experiences of each were very different. This was no stereotyped move of God. He had not dealt with everyone in the congregation in the same way. Some experienced the agony of deep conviction. Others were caught up with joy and praise. Others experienced in the midst of the noise a strange and beautiful peace. Some were sitting, others standing, some on their knees, others on their faces before God on the gravel floor. No response was identical. In all this I learned an important lesson about revival—even in the midst of a corporate move of God's Spirit across His people, He still deals with each one individually. Isn't that just like God? Even when He moves corporately, He still meets with us at our point of personal need.

Gradually the noise of people praying, crying and responding to God in various ways began to subside and the meeting came to a place of quiet again. Then Michael stepped forward, said a few words, we sang a song of worship and prayed and the service came to a close.

A Wall of Fire

Later I was talking with an old Solomon Island elder who had been a part of the revival in the Solomon Islands from its start in 1970. He said that in our meeting when the Holy Spirit was moving like a wave across the congregation, he was on the platform watching what was happening. He said as the wave of sound moved forward, he saw a vision of a wall of fire moving across the congregation. This was the Holy Spirit coming among us just like He did on the Day of Pentecost. And what happened at that Easter convention on Malaita Island was the beginning of a new wave of revival fire that spread across the island and to other regions of the Solomon Islands in the months that followed.

Our visit to the Solomon Islands lasted only three weeks (though I have been back many times since), and during that short time I saw and experienced the presence and power of God in ways I have never experienced it in all my years as a Christian, a missionary and a pastor. I went to the Solomon Islands with the prayer that I would not only witness revival there firsthand but would be touched by it and return with the fire of God in my heart. I know God answered my prayer—those three weeks changed my life forever!

Returning from the Solomon Islands, I felt a new anointing on my life and ministry that I had not known before. Three weeks in revival did something for me that thirty years as a Christian had not done: It focused my life and ministry in a new way on the essentials of the Christian life and stripped away all the baggage that had accumulated and cluttered my life over the years. It showed me so clearly that the central things of the Christian life are exactly what 2 Chronicles 7:14 talks about—living in humility, devoting time to prayer and seeking God's face, keeping my heart pure, loving Jesus above all else and learning to depend on the Holy Spirit in everything. Out of these core issues of life, everything else flows.

Notes

Chapter 1: The Fire of Revival

1. Cited in Selwyn Hughes, *Every Day with Jesus* (Sunbury, UK: Crusade for World Revival, 1989).

2. Ibid.

3. Vance Havner, *Hearts Afire* (Old Tappan, N.J.: Revell, 1952), 103–4.

4. J. Edwin Orr, *The Second Evangelical Awakening in Britain* (London: Marshall, Morgan & Scott, 1949).

5. Cited in Winnie Kemp, *Joseph W. Kemp* (London: Marshall, Morgan & Scott, 1936), 32–33.

6. James Burns, *Revival, Their Laws and Leaders* (Grand Rapids: Baker, 1960), 15.

Chapter 3: Our Greatest Problem—Pride

1. W. E. Sangster, *Revival—the Need and the Way* (London: Epworth Press, 1957), 42.

2. Quoted in D. Hartin, *God's Conditions for Revival* (Brisbane: Jollen Press, 1988), 15.

3. Ibid., 18.

4. L. E. Maxwell, *Born Crucified* (Chicago: Moody, 1945), 55.

5. Paul Smith, *Church Aflame* (London: Marshall, Morgan & Scott, 1953), 23.

Chapter 4: The First Condition—Humility

1. Duncan Campbell, *When the Mountains Flowed Down* (a taped message given to students of the Faith Mission Bible College, Edinburgh, Scotland, 1954).

2. Francis Frangipane, *The House of the Lord* (Milton Keynes: Word, 1991), 59.

Chapter 5: A Hunger for God's Presence

1. J. Greenfield, *Power from on High* (Edinburgh: Marshall, Morgan & Scott, 1927), 14.

2. Duncan Campbell, *The Lewis Awakening* (Edinburgh: Faith Mission, 1953), 14.

Chapter 7: The Marks of Revival Praying

1. Evan Roberts, quoted in James Stewart, *Invasion of Wales by the Spirit* (Ft. Washington, Pa.: Christian Literature Crusade, 1970).

2. Ibid.

3. Selwyn Hughes, *Every Day with Jesus* (Sunbury, UK: Crusade for World Revival, 1989).

4. Ibid.

Chapter 9: Substitutes for Intimacy

1. Wayne Jacobsen, *A Passion for God's Presence* (Eugene, Ore.: Harvest House, 1991), 52.

2. Richard Foster, *Celebration of Discipline* (London: Hodder & Stoughton, 1980), 19.

Chapter 11: Where Revival Begins

1. William Blair and Bruce Hunt, *The Korean Pentecost* (Carlisle, Pa.: Banner of Truth, 1977), 72–73.

2. A. W. Tozer, *Gems from Tozer* (Harrisburg, Pa.: Christian Publications, 1969), 84.

3. Shirley Lees, *Drunk Before Dawn* (Sevenoaks: OMF, 1979), 182–83.

4. Richard Lovelace, *Dynamics of Spiritual Life* (Downers Grove, Ill.: Inter-Varsity Press, 1979), 41.

5. Helen Hosier, *Jonathan Edwards—the Great Awakener* (Uhrichsville, Ohio: Barbour Publishing, 1998), 88.

6. Jonathan Goforth, *By My Spirit* (London: Marshall, Morgan & Scott, 1929), 185.

Chapter 12: Individual Repentance

1. Charles Finney, *How to Experience Revival* (Springdale, Pa.: Whitaker House, 1984), 28–29.
2. Evan Roberts in W. T. Stead, ed., *The Story of the Welsh Revival* (London: Fleming H. Revell, 1905), 6.

Chapter 13: Corporate Repentance

1. John Dawson, *Healing America's Wounds* (Ventura, Calif.: Regal Books, 1994), 15.

Chapter 14: Identificational Repentance

1. John Dawson, *Healing America's Wounds* (Ventura, Calif.: Regal Books, 1994), 246.
2. Ibid., 245–46.
3. Ibid., 79–80.

Chapter 15: What Should We Expect?

1. Alison Griffiths, *Fire in the Islands* (Wheaton: Harold Shaw, 1977), 175.
2. Brian Edwards, *Revival* (Darlington, UK: Evangelical Press, 1990), 140.
3. Martyn Lloyd-Jones, *The Puritans: Their Origins and Successors* (London: Banner of Truth, 1987), 1–2.
4. W. T. Stead, ed., *The Story of the Welsh Revival* (London: Fleming H. Revell, 1905).
5. George Strachan, *Revival—Its Blessings and Battles* (Sydney: Missions Publications of Australia, 1984), 1.

Chapter 16: The Fear of Revival

1. Jonathan Edwards, *Works of Jonathan Edwards* (New Haven: Yale University Press, 1959), 13.

Chapter 17: The Phenomena of Revival

1. John Wesley, *Journals of John Wesley* (London: Epworth Press, 1938), 51.

2. Richard Crisco, *It's Time* (Shippensburg, Pa.: Revival Press, 1997), 14–15.

3. Wesley, *Journals of John Wesley,* 54.

Chapter 18: A Revival of Prayer

1. Jessie Penn-Lewis, *The Awakening in Wales* (Dorset, UK: Overcomer Literature Trust, 1905), 55.

2. William Blair and Bruce Hunt, *The Korean Pentecost* (Carlisle, Pa.: Banner of Truth, 1977), 15.

Chapter 19: A Revival of Worship

1. Quoted in Brian Edwards, *Revival* (Darlington, UK: Evangelical Press, 1990), 142.

2. Rhys Bevan Jones, *Rent Heavens* (London: Pioneer Mission, 1931), 43.

3. Iain Murray, *The First Forty Years* (Edinburgh: Banner of Truth, 1982), 220.

4. Edwards, *Revival,* 146.

Chapter 20: Holiness and Harvest

1. Quoted in Brian Edwards, *Revival* (Darlington, UK: Evangelical Press, 1990), 137.

2. Quoted in Charles Crismier, *Renewing the Soul of America* (Richmond: Elijah Books, 2002).

Chapter 22: Why Revivals Die

1. Richard Lovelace, *Dynamics of Spiritual Life* (Downers Grove, Ill.: Inter-Varsity Press, 1979), 41.

Chapter 23: Revival and Discipleship

1. Mark Shaw, *Ten Great Ideas from Church History* (Downers Grove, Ill.: InterVarsity Press, 1997), 136.

2. Quoted in Thomas Jackson, *Centenary of Wesleyan Methodism* (New York: Abingdon Press, 1936), 69.

3. George Strachan, *Revival—Its Blessings and Battles* (Sydney: Missions Publications of Australia, 1984), 2–3.

Chapter 24: Preparation Begins at Home!

1. Quoted in Allan Peterson, ed., *The Marriage Affair* (Wheaton: Tyndale House, 1971), 191.

Chapter 25: The Power of Unity

1. Colombia story from the video *Transformations 1* (Global Net Productions, 1999).

2. From an article by J. Edwin Orr, "Prayer and Revival," *Renewal Journal* 1, no. 1 (1993): 13–18.

3. Some of these keys are found in Ed Silvoso, *That None Should Perish* (Ventura, Calif.: Regal Books, 1995), 239–40.

Chapter 26: "Lord, Do It Again!"

1. Winkie Pratney, *Revival* (Springdale, Pa.: Whitaker House, 1983), 7.

2. Brian Edwards, *Revival* (Darlington, UK: Evangelical Press, 1990), 23.

3. Steve May, *1001 Contemporary Illustrations* (Raleigh, N.C.: Heaven Word, 1999).

INDEX

 **Ian Malins** is a former missionary, Bible teacher, pastor and author. He and his wife, Diane, were Bible teachers on the staff of the Christian Leaders' Training College of Papua New Guinea for fourteen years, followed by ten years of pastoral ministry in churches in Queensland, Australia. Ian has ministered in the Solomon Islands over many years and experienced revival there firsthand. Both he and Diane are founders of Omega Discipleship Ministries and are now involved in a training and teaching ministry to the wider Body of Christ. They have three sons—Dallas, Peter and David.

Other Books by Ian Malins

Understanding Our Need of Revival
This exciting series of fifteen studies looks at what revival is, what God's intention is for His people and why we desperately need revival today. Includes stories from past revivals and questions for personal study and small group discussion.

Come Let Us Worship
In this life-changing series of twelve studies, Ian Malins looks at the importance and inner meaning of worship as a way of life, rather than as just an event on Sundays. Each study includes application projects and questions and is ideal for small groups.

Discipleship Series

1. *Come to Me*
Five studies explain in a clear and compelling way the basic message of Christianity and how to become a Christian. In a workbook format with study questions, this is an ideal tool to help you lead a person to Christ.

2. *My First Steps*
This series of twenty key studies covers the essential first steps in following Jesus and includes the five studies of *Come to Me*. Also in workbook format, this is a valuable tool for nurturing and discipling new believers.

3. *I Will Follow Jesus*
These seven studies are taken from *My First Steps* and are designed for those preparing for water baptism. The book places baptism in the context of the conversion process and touches on related areas of repentance, the Holy Spirit, spiritual warfare and commitment to the Body. Also in workbook format.

4. *Come Follow Me*
This clear and comprehensive series of sixty studies looks at what it means to be a true disciple, covering principles of growth, dangers to overcome, living under Christ's Lordship and the Spirit-filled life. Includes discussion questions and practical growth projects.

5. *Go and Make Disciples*
These 27 studies teach key concepts and practical principles in the areas of witnessing, nurturing new believers, mentoring, discipling others and world mission. The book is an exciting training manual showing how to use *Come to Me* and *My First Steps* as evangelistic and discipling tools.

6. *Leader's Manual*
This handbook for churches and group leaders outlines how to begin discipleship training and provides leaders with guidelines on how to use each book in the series.

Books available from:
Omega Discipleship Ministries
Web site: www.omega-discipleship.com
E-mail: contact@omega-discipleship.com